PROCESSES THAT SHAPE THE EARTH

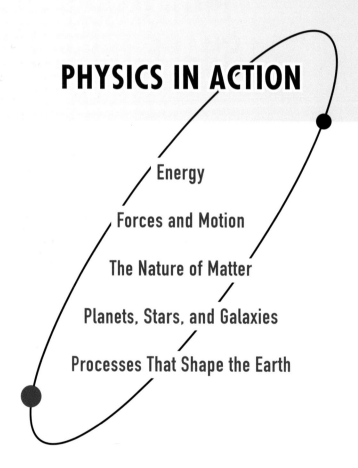

PHYSICS IN ACTION

Energy

Forces and Motion

The Nature of Matter

Planets, Stars, and Galaxies

Processes That Shape the Earth

PHYSICS in ACTION

PROCESSES THAT SHAPE THE EARTH

David M. Thompson

Series Editor
David G. Haase

CHELSEA HOUSE
PUBLISHERS
An imprint of Infobase Publishing

Processes That Shape the Earth

Copyright © 2007 by Infobase Publishing

All rights reserved. No part of this book may be reproduced or utilized in any form or by any means, electronic or mechanical, including photocopying, recording, or by any information storage or retrieval systems, without permission in writing from the publisher. For information contact:

Chelsea House
An imprint of Infobase Publishing
132 West 31st Street
New York NY 10001

Library of Congress Cataloging-in-Publication Data
Thompson, David M. (David Mattoon), 1977-
  Processes that shape the earth / David M. Thompson.
     p. cm. — (Physics in action)
  Includes bibliographical references and index.
  ISBN-13: 978-0-7910-8932-3 (hardcover)
  ISBN-10: 0-7910-8932-0 (hardcover)
  1. Physical geology—Juvenile literature. I. Title. II. Series.

  QE28.2.T46 2007
  551—dc22

                              2007008794

Chelsea House books are available at special discounts when purchased in bulk quantities for businesses, associations, institutions, or sales promotions. Please call our Special Sales Department in New York at (212) 967-8800 or (800) 322-8755.

You can find Chelsea House on the World Wide Web at http://www.chelseahouse.com

Text design by James Scotto-Lavino
Cover design by Takeshi Takahashi

Printed in the United States of America

Bang FOF 10 9 8 7 6 5 4 3 2 1

This book is printed on acid-free paper.

All links and Web addresses were checked and verified to be correct at the time of publication. Because of the dynamic nature of the Web, some addresses and links may have changed since publication and may no longer be valid.

CONTENTS

CHAPTER 1

Introduction to Physical Geology

THE WORD GEOLOGY DERIVES FROM THE GREEK WORDS "GEO," meaning Earth, and "logia," meaning study. **Geology** is literally the study of the Earth, and those who study the Earth are called geologists. Many people imagine that geologists only study rocks, but this is far from true. Geologists can be found collecting gases from a volcano, using radar to look beneath the desert sands, drilling holes miles deep into ice, and mapping the ocean floor with sound. The quest to understand the workings of our planet takes geologists to some of its most remote locations.

Humans have studied the Earth for thousands of years. The ancient Greeks were among the first to ask basic questions such as, "What is the Earth's shape?" Today, with a globe in almost every classroom, everyone knows the Earth is shaped like a sphere. But thousands of years ago, the answer to this question was far less obvious.

It was in the fourth century B.C. that Aristotle succeeded in proving that the Earth is spherical. He arrived at this conclusion not by studying the rocks at his feet, but by studying shadows on the moon. During a lunar eclipse, the Earth and moon are aligned so that the Earth casts a shadow on the moon. Aristotle noted that this shadow is always circular, and the only shape that always casts a circular shadow is a sphere.

Other early geologists also made important discoveries about the Earth. In 250 B.C., Eratosthenes carefully measured the angle of sunlight at two different locations and correctly calculated the size of the Earth. In the fifteenth century, Leonardo da Vinci discovered, by studying layers of dirt, that the Earth must be at least hundreds of thousands of years old.

Although these earliest geologists learned a great deal, some of their work was later forgotten. Hundreds of years ago, the Catholic Church was far more powerful than today, and it could imprison people whose views were considered unholy. In particular, the Catholic Church banned scientific results that conflicted with the Bible. The Church especially disliked geology because a careful study of the Earth could disprove the Bible's story of a six-day creation. Shunning science, Church leaders promoted the work of a man named James Ussher.

In the 1600s, Ussher carefully combed the Bible for information on the Earth's creation. He concluded, much to the delight of the Catholic Church, that the Earth was created on Saturday, October 22, 4004 B.C., at around 6 p.m. While this result sounds absurd to a modern reader, it was taken seriously by many people. When pressed to explain how all the mountains and valleys could have been made in only 6,000 years, religious philosophers invented **catastrophism**. The incorrect theory of catastrophism claims that the Earth's features were shaped by major catastrophes, like the gigantic flood in the story of Noah and his ark.

In the 1700s, the theory of Biblical catastrophism was overturned by James Hutton, the celebrated "father of modern geology." He replaced catastrophism with the principle of **uniformitarianism**. According to the principle of uniformitarianism, the slow processes at work on Earth today are the same processes that have acted on the Earth in the past. Places like Mount Everest and the Grand Canyon were made by the same kinds of changes that are happening today. Over millions of years, the slow movement of the continents makes mountains. Over equally long times, erosion by rivers makes valleys. To better understand how these mountains and valleys were made in the past, Hutton said that we should study what is happening on the Earth *right now.* This theory of uniformitarianism is famously summarized by the statement that "the present is the key to the past."

Geology now has two main branches: **historical geology** and **physical geology**. Historical geology is the study of Earth's history. Physical geology is the study of the physics, or processes, that shape the Earth. The main topic of this book is the field of physical geology. Of course, physical and historical geology are so closely related that it is impossible to study one without learning something about the other, so some discussion of the Earth's history is included here as well. We begin, in Chapter 2, with a general overview of planet Earth. After a brief discussion of the Earth's formation, Chapter 2 introduces the Earth's sources of energy and the cycles powered by that energy. The two most

JAMES HUTTON: The Father of Modern Geology

At the time of James Hutton's birth in 1726, most scholars believed the Earth to be no more than 6,000 years old, in line with biblical teachings. Less than 60 years later, Hutton disproved the conventional wisdom and revolutionized the study of the Earth.

In 1784, Hutton presented his theory of the Earth in a series of lectures. He argued that sediments erode off the land, settle on the sea floor, and then turn to rock. Forces from below the crust push this newly formed rock above sea level to become dry land. This new land also undergoes erosion, sending its sediments back into the sea to complete the cycle. (This is part of the rock cycle: Follow the path back and forth between sediments and sedimentary rock in Figure 2.3.) By measuring the incredibly slow rate of this cycle, Hutton was able to prove that the Earth was much older than 6,000 years.

important sources of energy are the Earth's internal heat and the heat delivered by sunlight.

The Earth's internal heat causes the continents to move; exactly how this happens is described by the theory of plate tectonics, which is one of the most important ideas in all of modern geology. Plate tectonics is discussed in Chapter 3. Aside from explaining the formation of mountains and oceans, plate tectonics also plays an important role in the creation and destruction of rocks, which are the topics of Chapter 4.

Sunlight, the other main source of Earth's energy, powers the rain that delivers water from the oceans to the land in a cycle described in Chapter 5. At times in the past, however, the Earth has been much colder than today. During the Ice Age, described in Chapter 6, much more of the atmosphere's water fell on the land as snow instead of rain, creating gigantic chunks of ice called **glaciers**. The glaciers of the Ice Age played a large role in shaping the landscape of Canada, northern Europe, and the northern United States. The physics of glaciers and their effect on the land is described in Chapter 7.

The sun also produces wind by heating the air. Chapter 8 describes how the wind creates distinctive features on land. The wind, in turn, produces waves on the ocean, and those waves shape the shoreline in various processes discussed in Chapter 9. Finally, Chapter 10 describes how humans have become the dominant force at work on the Earth today. Powered by fossil fuels, humans have reshaped the land's surface and altered the composition of the atmosphere.

CHAPTER 2

Overview of Planet Earth

THE UNIVERSE BEGAN WITH A BIG EXPLOSION ABOUT 13 BILLION years ago. For lack of a better name, scientists call this the **Big Bang**. Before the Big Bang, there was no light, there were no atoms, nor was there even any space or time. The Big Bang created only the three lightest elements: hydrogen, helium, and lithium. In the beginning, the universe was filled with clouds of these three elements and nothing else. How, then, did carbon, oxygen, and all of the other elements get created? Before answering that question, we will first review some facts about atoms.

ELEMENTS AND ISOTOPES

All atoms can be described by two pieces of information: the atomic number and the isotope. The **atomic number** is the number of protons contained in an atom's nucleus. An element—such as hydrogen, carbon, or oxygen—is a group of atoms that all have the same atomic number. For example, every hydrogen atom has atomic number one, every helium atom has atomic number two, and so on.

Although all the atoms that belong to the same element have the same number of protons, they do not necessarily have the same number of neutrons. An **isotope** is a subgroup of an element in which the atoms do have the same number of neutrons. The most common isotope of hydrogen has no neutrons; its nucleus is just a single proton. However, there is also a rare isotope of hydrogen that does have a neutron; its nucleus is made of one proton and one neutron that are stuck together.

The elements produced during the Big Bang—hydrogen, helium, and lithium—are highlighted in blue in Figure 2.1. In contrast, the major elements of the Earth are highlighted in orange.

FORMATION OF THE EARTH

Getting back to the original question, where did all of the other elements come from? The elements of atomic number greater than three were created by stars. Inside our own star, the sun, hydrogen atoms are smashed together to make helium atoms. This is the same reaction that occurs within modern nuclear weapons. As stars get older, they begin smashing together helium atoms to make elements with higher atomic numbers.

When a star gets too old, it may die in a violent explosion. When the ancient stars exploded, they scattered their brand-new elements throughout space. This left the universe filled with clouds of elements like carbon and oxygen, which are vital for life, and other elements, like iron and silicon, that are found in abundance on Earth. Slowly but surely, gravity pulled these clouds back together to form new stars, like our sun. The sun was created by a collapsing cloud roughly 5 billion years ago.

Some parts of this cloud were moving too fast to be sucked into the sun. These atoms formed an orbiting disk. Atoms in this disk clumped together to form dust, and pieces of dust stuck together to make even larger pieces. Over time, these clumps of matter collected into large masses called planets; the Earth was formed in this way.

Our moon was formed in a slightly different way. In the early years, a small planet crashed into the Earth. The collision was so forceful that a chunk of the Earth was catapulted into space. That chunk became the moon.

Periodic Table of the Elements

Atomic number — 3
Symbol — Li
Atomic weight — 6.941

1 IA																	18 VIIIA
1 H 1.00794	2 IIA											13 IIIA	14 IVA	15 VA	16 VIA	17 VIIA	2 He 4.0026
3 Li 6.941	4 Be 9.0122											5 B 10.81	6 C 12.011	7 N 14.0067	8 O 15.9994	9 F 18.9984	10 Ne 20.1798
11 Na 22.9898	12 Mg 24.3051	3 IIIB	4 IVB	5 VB	6 VIB	7 VIIB	8 VIIIB	9 VIIIB	10 VIIIB	11 IB	12 IIB	13 Al 26.9815	14 Si 28.0855	15 P 30.9738	16 S 32.067	17 Cl 35.4528	18 Ar 39.948
19 K 39.0938	20 Ca 40.078	21 Sc 44.9559	22 Ti 47.867	23 V 50.9415	24 Cr 51.9962	25 Mn 54.938	26 Fe 55.845	27 Co 58.9332	28 Ni 58.6934	29 Cu 63.546	30 Zn 65.409	31 Ga 69.723	32 Ge 72.61	33 As 74.9216	34 Se 78.96	35 Br 79.904	36 Kr 83.798
37 Rb 85.4678	38 Sr 87.62	39 Y 88.906	40 Zr 91.224	41 Nb 92.9064	42 Mo 95.94	43 Tc (98)	44 Ru 101.07	45 Rh 102.9055	46 Pd 106.42	47 Ag 107.8682	48 Cd 112.412	49 In 114.818	50 Sn 118.711	51 Sb 121.760	52 Te 127.60	53 I 126.9045	54 Xe 131.29
55 Cs 132.9054	56 Ba 137.328	57-70 ☆	72 Hf 178.49	73 Ta 180.948	74 W 183.84	75 Re 186.207	76 Os 190.23	77 Ir 192.217	78 Pt 195.08	79 Au 196.9655	80 Hg 200.59	81 Tl 204.3833	82 Pb 207.2	83 Bi 208.9804	84 Po (209)	85 At (210)	86 Rn (222)
87 Fr (223)	88 Ra (226)	89-102 ★	104 Rf (261)	105 Db (262)	106 Sg (266)	107 Bh (262)	108 Hs (263)	109 Mt (268)	110 Ds (271)	111 Rg (272)	112 Uub (277)						

☆ Lanthanoids

57 La 138.9055	58 Ce 140.115	59 Pr 140.908	60 Nd 144.24	61 Pm (145)	62 Sm 150.36	63 Eu 151.966	64 Gd 157.25	65 Tb 158.9253	66 Dy 162.500	67 Ho 164.9303	68 Er 167.26	69 Tm 168.9342	70 Yb 173.04

★ Actinoids

89 Ac (227)	90 Th 232.0381	91 Pa 231.036	92 U 238.0289	93 Np (237)	94 Pu (244)	95 Am 243	96 Cm (247)	97 Bk (247)	98 Cf (251)	99 Es (252)	100 Fm (257)	101 Md (258)	102 No (259)

Numbers in parentheses are atomic mass numbers of most stable isotopes.

© Infobase Publishing

Figure 2.1 *The Big Bang produced the three elements highlighted in blue on the periodic table, while the Earth is composed primarily of the elements colored in orange.*

After the formation of the moon, a bombardment of smaller meteorites continued to add mass to the Earth and moon. By about 4.5 billion years ago, most of the meteorites had been swept up by the orbiting planets, and the Earth and moon were the size they are today.

SOURCES OF ENERGY

The Earth's energy comes from two main sources: light from the sun and heat from within the Earth itself. The sun is the most obvious source of energy and also the most powerful, delivering an average of 342 watts per square meter over the Earth's surface. A watt (W) is a unit of power, which is energy per time. For comparison, a standard lightbulb uses 60 watts of power.

The other source of energy, called **geothermal** energy, is the heat emanating from deep inside the Earth. Some of this heat was built up during the formation of the Earth and has been slowly escaping ever since. An even more important source of geothermal energy comes from radioactive decay, the natural process by which an atom spontaneously emits particles from its nucleus. Most naturally occurring isotopes do not undergo radioactive decay. The isotopes that do are referred to as **radioactive**.

The Earth contains three important radioactive isotopes: isotopes of uranium, thorium, and potassium. When these isotopes decay, they give off energy that contributes to Earth's geothermal heat. (We will discuss radioactive decay in more detail in Chapter 6.) Geothermal heat escapes to the Earth's surface at a rate of 0.06 watts per square meter. This may seem like a small amount of energy, especially compared to the 342 W/m^2 from the sun, but this energy drives many important processes.

A third source of power for the Earth is tidal energy. The tides are generated by the gravitational interaction with the moon. This will be discussed in more detail in Chapter 9.

LAYERS AND "SPHERES"

At the very center of the Earth is the **core**, a spherical ball of iron. As you might expect, the core is very heavy: It has an average density of

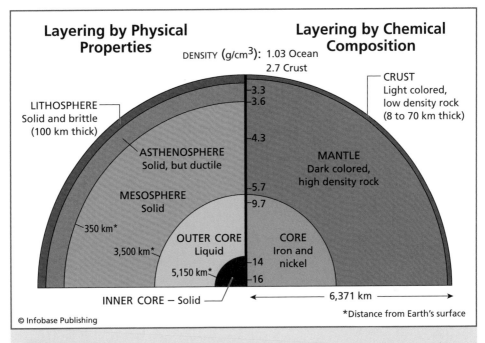

Layering by Physical Properties

Layering by Chemical Composition

DENSITY (g/cm³): 1.03 Ocean
2.7 Crust

CRUST
Light colored,
low density rock
(8 to 70 km thick)

LITHOSPHERE
Solid and brittle
(100 km thick)

—3.3
—3.6

—4.3

ASTHENOSPHERE
Solid, but ductile

MANTLE
Dark colored,
high density rock

MESOSPHERE
Solid

—5.7
—9.7

350 km*

OUTER CORE
Liquid

CORE
Iron and
nickel

3,500 km*

5,150 km*

—14
—16

INNER CORE — Solid

← 6,371 km →

*Distance from Earth's surface

© Infobase Publishing

Figure 2.2 *The layers of the Earth are shown here with compositional layers on the right and the physical layers on the left.*

11 grams per cubic centimeter. The core is four times as dense as the rocks on Earth's surface, which have an average density of 2.7 g/cm³. For comparison, keep in mind that water has a density of 1 g/cm³.

Above the core are two layers made out of silicate rock, which is rock composed of silicon and oxygen, two of the most common elements on the Earth. The two silicate layers above the core are the **mantle** in the middle and the **crust** on the outside. Although the crust and mantle are both made of silicate rock, the crust is distinguished from the mantle because it is less dense.

Since the crust in the continents is of different composition, density, and thickness than the crust underneath the oceans, the Earth's crust is often subdivided into continental crust and oceanic crust. The oceanic crust is only 8 kilometers (5 miles) thick. The continental crust is thicker, ranging from 25 to 70 kilometers

(15.5 to 43.5 miles) deep. As shown in Figure 2.2, the crust is much thinner than either the core or the mantle, which are thousands of kilometers thick.

The layers just described are a good way to picture what the Earth is made of: dense iron (the core), medium-density silicate (the mantle), and light silicate (the crust). However, to describe how the Earth moves, we must define a different set of layers. Geologists define the **lithosphere** as the entire crust and the top part of the mantle. Below the lithosphere is a part of the mantle called the **asthenosphere**. Both of these layers are subsets of the crust and mantle, so they are made of silicate rock. The difference between the two is that the asthenosphere is soft and the lithosphere is rigid. It might sound weird to think of rock as being "soft," but the asthenosphere is so hot that the rock can actually flow.

The rigid lithosphere does not have a uniform thickness. Underneath the ocean, it is only slightly thicker than the crust: It includes the crust and only a few kilometers of the mantle. On land, the lithosphere can be much thicker, encompassing a couple hundred kilometers of the mantle. In general, the lithosphere acts like a hard layer that floats on top of the fluid-like asthenosphere.

Taken collectively, all the layers from the core to the rocky surface are called the geosphere. The Earth may be divided into four abstract "spheres" of matter: the geosphere, the biosphere, the hydrosphere, and the atmosphere. The geosphere is by far the largest of these. The biosphere is the smallest, although it contains all organic matter, both living and dead. Trees, pets, humans, and food all belong to the biosphere.

The hydrosphere consists of all water on top of or inside Earth's surface: oceans, lakes, rivers, snow, ice, and groundwater (but not water vapor in the atmosphere). It is not difficult to guess that most of the Earth's water, 97%, resides in the oceans. However, it may come as a surprise to learn that there is hundreds of times more water in ice and groundwater than there is in all the lakes and rivers, which contain only 0.01% of all of Earth's water.

The atmosphere consists of all the air above the Earth's surface, including nitrogen, oxygen, argon, water vapor, and carbon dioxide. Nitrogen (78%) and oxygen (21%) make up about 99% of all the dry air in the atmosphere. Although carbon dioxide makes up less than 0.1% of the atmosphere, it has a huge impact on the Earth's climate, as will be discussed in Chapter 10.

THE ROCK CYCLE

From a geological perspective, diamonds are *not* forever. In fact, rocks and minerals are constantly being created, transformed, and destroyed. Together, these processes are called the **rock cycle**. Rocks are grouped into three types: **igneous**, **sedimentary**, and **metamorphic**. The precursor to all rock is **magma**, which is a form of rock that is so hot that it is liquid-like or molten. The familiar form of magma is lava, which is the name given to magma when it has been brought to the Earth's surface.

Igneous rock is formed when magma cools into a rigid solid. Igneous rock is further classified as intrusive or extrusive, based on how it was formed. When a volcano erupts and its lava cools on the surface, the resulting rock is called **extrusive**. Lightweight pumice, which cools faster than bubbles of gas can escape, is an example of extrusive igneous rock. **Intrusive** rock is made when magma cools slowly inside the Earth. **Granite** is an example of intrusive igneous rock.

Sedimentary rock forms when loose material, like sand and dirt, combines into solid rock. This kind of rock is called sedimentary because deposits of fine, loose material are called **sediments**. The formation of sedimentary rock can occur when sediment is buried so deeply that it becomes compressed into rock by high pressures. Sedimentary rock can also be formed when naturally occurring chemicals glue the grains of sediment together. The general process of turning sediments into sedimentary rock is called **lithification**, and it will be discussed in detail in Chapter 4.

Metamorphic rock is the name given to igneous or sedimentary rock after it has been changed by high temperatures or pressures. This happens when the rock has been buried deep inside the Earth. When a geologist identifies a piece of metamorphic rock, he or she knows that the rock has made a long journey up to the surface.

The rock cycle is the movement of matter among five groups: magma, igneous rock, sediment, sedimentary rock, and metamor-

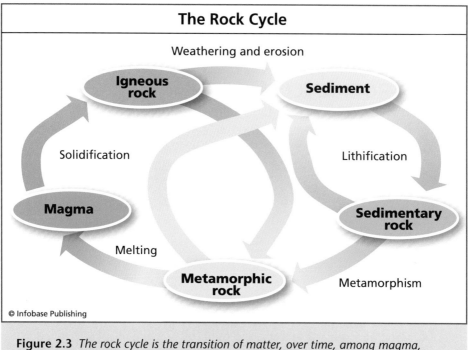

Figure 2.3 *The rock cycle is the transition of matter, over time, among magma, igneous rock, sediment, sedimentary rock, and metamorphic rock.*

phic rock. As an example, follow the outer path in Figure 2.3. Starting on the left-hand side, *magma* cools into *igneous rock*. As the igneous rock erodes into tiny pieces, layers of *sediment* gather on the Earth's surface. When the sediment is buried deep in the Earth, it gets compressed into *sedimentary rock*. And, if that sedimentary rock should get heated up, it may transform into *metamorphic rock*. Finally, if the rock gets so hot that it melts, it once again becomes *magma*. Every rock on Earth has followed some path in Figure 2.3 to become what it is today.

OTHER CYCLES

There are many cycles at work on the Earth. One of the most noticeable is the **hydrologic cycle**, which is the water cycle. Water is continually on the move between various reservoirs—ocean water, groundwater, ice, and surface water. All of this movement is powered by the sun, which evaporates water to make clouds.

If the clouds rain over land, the water may flow back to the ocean through rivers, or it may evaporate again to form other clouds. The water may even enter the biosphere through the roots of plants. This cycle of freshwater will be discussed in detail in Chapter 5. Sometimes, the clouds release their water in the form of snow. Near the poles of the Earth or atop high mountains, the water can remain as ice for thousands of years before being released back to the ocean. The behavior of this ice and its impact on the landscape is covered in Chapter 7.

Without the hydrologic cycle, animals and plants on land would have no access to water. The carbon cycle is equally important for life, because carbon is the fundamental building block of all living things. The atmosphere contains carbon in the form of carbon dioxide: This is a molecule with one carbon atom and two oxygen atoms, written as CO_2. In the carbon cycle, plants absorb CO_2 from the atmosphere, use the carbon to make the substances they need for growth, and release the leftover oxygen. Animals eat the carbon-based plants and inhale oxygen from the air. Inside the animals' bodies, the carbon and oxygen are combined to make carbon dioxide, which is exhaled back to the atmosphere. This loop between plants, animals, and the atmosphere is the central part of the carbon cycle.

CHAPTER 3

Plate Tectonics

O N THE EARTH, SOME CHANGES TAKE PLACE IN MINUTES, WHILE others take millions of years. The fast changes are easy to recognize. The sun rises and sets every day, and the seasons progress through their cycles every year. These changes are short enough that a single human can experience them in a lifetime.

Other changes on Earth, especially those studied by geologists, take place much more slowly. Among the slowest of these is the movement of the ground beneath our feet. Because this process is so slow, it was a while before scientists even recognized it was happening.

EVIDENCE FOR PLATE TECTONICS

Over the past two centuries, many people had noticed that South America and Africa look like two interlocking pieces of a jigsaw puzzle. Despite this, no one investigated the observation in detail. No one, that is, until Alfred Wegener.

In 1915, Wegener published a groundbreaking text titled *The Origin of Continents and Oceans*. In it, he argued that South America and Africa had once been joined together. In fact, he proposed that *all* of today's landmasses were once part of a gigantic continent called Pangaea. Over the course of millions of years, he said, Pangaea broke up and the pieces drifted to their current positions today.

In search of evidence for his theory, Wegener studied fossils from South America and Africa. As Wegener discovered, some of the fossils found in Africa were identical to the fossils found in South America. This meant that the same plants and animals were living in both places at the same time. This could be explained in two ways: Either the plants and animals crossed the ocean, or the continents were once joined together.

Wegener argued that some of the plants and animals could not have crossed the ocean. One of the plants had seeds that were too large to have been blown that far. One of the animals, an alligator-like reptile, lived only in freshwater. It never could have survived a trip through the salty ocean. Only one explanation made sense—that South America and Africa had been joined together, and only later did they drift apart.

Today, we have direct evidence for **continental drift**, which is the movement of the continents in relation to one another. As scientists have discovered, continental drift is not just something that happened long ago, but it is still occurring today and can be measured using the Global Positioning System (GPS). The GPS is a collection of 30 satellites in orbit around Earth, each of which broadcasts a unique signal. A GPS receiver, which picks up and deciphers these signals, can be bought as a small hand-held device. The farther the receiver is from a satellite, the longer it takes that satellite's signal to reach it. By measuring the tiny signal delays from at least four satellites, the GPS receiver pinpoints its position. Scientists have placed these GPS receivers at several locations around the Earth; this has allowed them to measure the positions of the continents to within a millimeter, which is the thickness of a dime. By recording the positions of the receivers through time, the velocity of the continents can be measured. For example, this is how geologists know that Hawaii is cruising towards Japan at a speed of 8.3 centimeters (3.3 inches) per year.

HOW PLATES MOVE

Alfred Wegener's theory of continental drift was not accepted immediately. Most scientists rejected the theory because they could not think of a way for the landmasses to move. The continents are, after all, gigantic slabs of rock. How could they plow through the solid rock of the seafloor?

One part of the answer is that the lithosphere floats on the asthenosphere. Recall that the lithosphere is the outermost layer of rigid rock. The lithosphere is thick in some places and thin in others. Although it might sound backwards at first, the thicker segments float *higher* than the thinner parts. To picture this, imagine blocks of wood of different sizes floating in water. Although the thicker blocks reach deeper into the water, they also rise higher above the surface. Likewise, the thicker a piece of lithosphere, the higher it will float.

Even given that the lithosphere floats, there was no guarantee that it could move. In fact, there was a good reason to believe that it could not. The Earth is entirely covered by big chunks of lithosphere called **plates**: seven big plates and several smaller ones. These plates are so tightly interlocked—like pieces of a spherical jigsaw puzzle—that there is no way for a plate to move without immediately bumping into a neighboring plate. To move at all, the plate would have to push under or over its neighbor. There would also have to be a way to fill the gap created on the other side. In Wegener's time, there was no reason to believe this was possible.

In the 1960s, geologists found the answer under the ocean. By then, scientists had collected detailed maps of the seafloor, and these maps revealed gigantic mountain ranges underneath the oceans. One of these mountain ranges runs down the middle of the Atlantic Ocean, and the other runs down the middle of the Pacific Ocean (Figure 3.1). They are called the **mid-ocean ridges**.

If we were to drain the oceans, the mid-ocean ridges would be some of the most prominent features on Earth. Climbers in this water-less world would find that the mid-ocean ridges also have a peculiar shape. Each mid-ocean ridge is really *two* ridges parallel

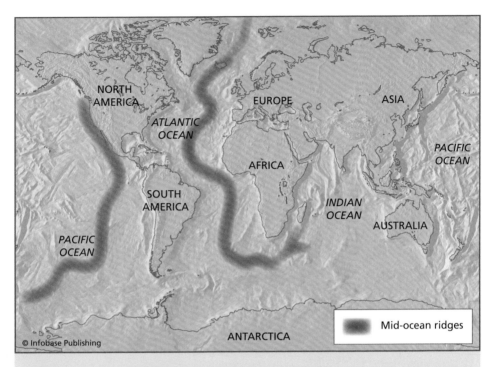

Figure 3.1 *This is a topographic map of the Earth with the oceans drained. The mid-ocean ridges feature prominently, running down the center of the Atlantic and Pacific.*

to each other. In between is a deep rift valley, which looks like a crack running down the length of the mid-ocean ridge.

In 1960, a Princeton University geologist named Harry Hess figured out how the plates are able to move. He proposed a mechanism for continental drift known as **seafloor spreading**. The rift valley, he argued, is the gap made by the two plates as they move away from each other. Magma continually rises up into the rift and cools onto the edges of the plates, effectively creating new ocean crust and preventing the rift valley from growing any larger. In order to explain how crust gets destroyed, Hess argued that the edges of some plates *do* push under and over each other. This elegant theory of seafloor spreading has since been proven by the careful study of the ocean floor and, more recently, with the GPS.

HARRY HESS: A Wartime Scientist

In 1941, at the beginning of World War II, Professor Harry Hess was called to duty. As an officer in the U.S. Navy Reserve, Lieutenant Hess tracked enemy submarines during the first half of the war and later commanded an attack transport vessel in four beach invasions, including the landing at Iwo Jima.

While serving as commanding officer of the USS *Cape Johnson*, Hess used the ship's echo sounder to map the height of the ocean floor along his routes. Through this wartime science, Hess discovered several flat-topped volcanoes below the ocean surface. He named these "guyots" in honor of Arnold Guyot, the founder of the Princeton University geology department.

Seafloor spreading is powered by geothermal heat. But what is heat? And how can heat make the lithosphere move? Heat is a disorganized form of energy in which molecules move randomly; the hotter a substance, the faster its molecules move. Although heat is random movement, an engine can harness heat to make organized motion. In a car, for example, the heat generated by burning gasoline (disorganized motion) is used to make the car move forwards (organized motion). When gasoline is reacted with the oxygen in air, the hot gas expands and pushes a piston that turns the wheels of the car.

Of course, there is no such engine inside the Earth. The "engine" of seafloor spreading relies on two facts:

1. When matter gets hot, it expands and becomes less dense.
2. Because of gravity, low-density matter rises and high-density matter sinks.

The result of these two facts is a process called **convection**. This process is familiar to anyone who has seen a burning candle. No matter how the candle itself is oriented, the candle flame always points away from the center of the Earth. This happens thanks to convection: The hot gases that make up the flame are *lighter* than the surrounding air, so they rise. In contrast, the cold air from a freezer is *denser* than the surrounding air, so it sinks to the kitchen floor. (Test this by putting your hands directly above and below an open freezer.)

When pockets of mantle rock get hot, their density decreases and they convect upwards from the Earth's core. Once the hot material reaches the bottom of the lithosphere, some of its heat passes through to the surface—this is the 0.06 watts per square meter

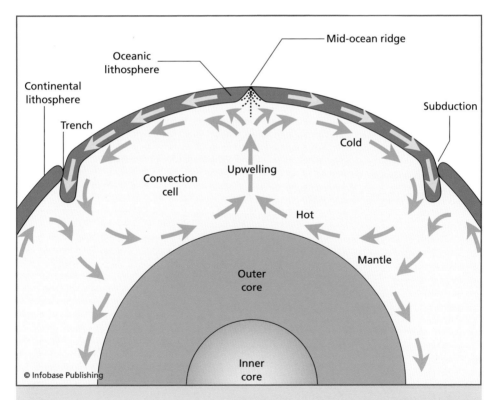

Figure 3.2 *Convection of mantle material drags the lithosphere along with it, powering plate tectonics.*

mentioned in Chapter 2. By passing heat through the lithosphere, the mantle rock cools, becomes denser, and sinks back towards the center of the Earth. This convection produces a flow of mantle rock along the bottom of the lithosphere. As the mantle material flows, it pushes on the lithospheric plates, causing them to move. A depiction of this process is shown in Figure 3.2. Of course, mantle rock flows very slowly, and, therefore, so do the plates. The plates move, on average, only a few centimeters per year.

PLATE MARGINS

The modern theory of plate movements and the plate margins is known as the theory of **plate tectonics**. For every bit of new seafloor created at a rift valley, an equal amount must be destroyed somewhere else. Both creation and destruction occur at the edges, or margins, of plates.

New lithosphere is made at **divergent margins**, such as the mid-ocean ridges, where the edges of plates move away from each other. Lithosphere is destroyed at **convergent margins**. This is where the margins of plates move towards each other. If two plates are sliding past each other, neither creating nor destroying any lithosphere, the line separating the two is called a **transform fault** margin.

Divergent Margins

Divergent margins occur in two types: on land and in the ocean. We have already discussed the mid-ocean ridges in the ocean. The mid-ocean ridge in the Atlantic is called the Mid-Atlantic Ridge. On either side of this ridge, the two plates move away from each other at a steady pace of 2 to 4 centimeters (0.8 to 1.6 inches) per year. The Atlantic Ocean is literally growing.

But what happens if we run time backwards? At a rate of 2 centimeters (0.8 inches) per year, the Atlantic Ocean must have been nonexistent roughly 100 million years ago. In fact, this is just about right. About 200 million years ago, there was no Atlantic Ocean—all of the major continents were joined together into the ancient continent of Pangaea. Thus, the Mid-Atlantic Ridge began as a divergent margin *on land*. Between 200 million and 165 million years ago, a divergent margin developed on Pangaea at the modern boundaries of Africa and South America. As the plates grew apart, the rift that divided them was filled with ocean water, giving birth to the Atlantic.

Today, this process is on display in the Great Rift Valley of Africa. At this divergent margin on land, the eastern edge of Africa is splitting away from the main part of the continent. As the two parts separate, magma fills in the void. Since this new crust is thinner than the surrounding crust, freshwater has accumulated in the depressions, making lakes. If the process were to continue, the African Rift Valley would eventually fill with sea water. The same process created the Red Sea, which continues to grow today as the Arabian plate moves away from the African plate.

Not all land rifts succeed in becoming oceans. About 1.1 billion years ago, a rift developed from Lake Superior to Kansas. This rift never succeeded in splitting the continent. Scientists are not sure what makes some rifts continue while others stop.

Convergent Margins

Since lithosphere can be either oceanic or continental, there are three possible pairings of plates at convergent margins: oceanic versus oceanic, oceanic versus continental, and continental versus continental. In the first two pairings, the oceanic lithosphere gets pushed underneath the neighboring plate and is recycled back into the mantle. This type of margin is called a **subduction zone**.

Once all the available oceanic crust at the subduction zone has been pushed into the mantle, only continental crust remains. This results in a continental-versus-continental convergent margin, which is called a **collision zone**.

Subduction Zones   As just noted, subduction zones come in two types: oceanic versus oceanic, or oceanic versus continental. The Aleutian Islands in Alaska were created by an oceanic versus oceanic subduction zone, and the Andes Mountains in South America were formed by an oceanic versus continental subduction zone. We will consider both examples in turn.

Just south of the Aleutian Islands, the oceanic crust of the Pacific Plate is forced under the oceanic crust of the North American plate (Figure 3.3a). As the Pacific plate dives into the mantle,

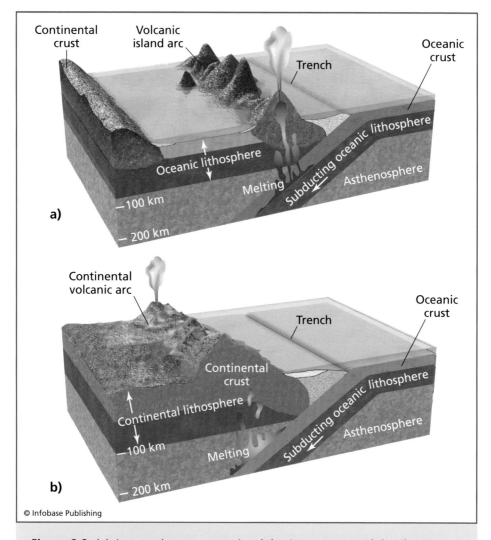

© Infobase Publishing

Figure 3.3 *(a) An oceanic-versus-oceanic subduction zone created the Aleutian Islands in Alaska, and (b) an oceanic-versus-continental subduction zone created the Andes Mountains in South America.*

the sea floor gets pulled down into a long, deep trench. Trenches formed at subduction zones are the deepest places on Earth.

As the oceanic crust subducts into the asthenosphere, the friction and the release of water from the crust causes rock to melt. This melted rock is less dense than the surrounding material, so it rises up through the overlying lithosphere and erupts at the surface as a volcano. This makes a string of volcanoes called a **volcanic arc**. In Alaska, the volcanic arc rises up out of the ocean to form the Aleutian Islands.

The western edge of South America provides a good example of an oceanic-versus-continental subduction zone. Here, the oceanic crust of the Nazca plate plunges underneath the South American plate right at the edge of the South American continent (Figure 3.3b). The force of the subducting Nazca plate pushes on the edge of the South American continent, causing the edge of the lithosphere to bunch up and rise into the sky. The result, in this case, is the Andes Mountains. Just as in oceanic-versus-oceanic subduction, water and friction cause buoyant magma to penetrate the edge of South America, dotting the Andes with volcanoes.

Collision Zones   Recall that the continental crust is thicker and lighter than the oceanic crust. Because of this, continental crust floats high on the asthenosphere. When two pieces of continental crust meet each other at a convergent margin, neither is thin enough to be pushed underneath the other. The result is that the two smash up against each other, eventually halting the convergence of the two plates. For example, India used to be part of Antarctica before it broke off and slowly moved north. About 45 million years ago, India collided with the Eurasian plate. Mount Everest, the tallest mountain in the world, was pushed up into the sky at this collision zone.

Transform Fault Margins

Taking a close look at Figure 3.4, which shows the tectonic plates, you will notice that the mid-ocean ridge in the Atlantic is not really one continuous ridge. Instead, it is a string of ridges that are

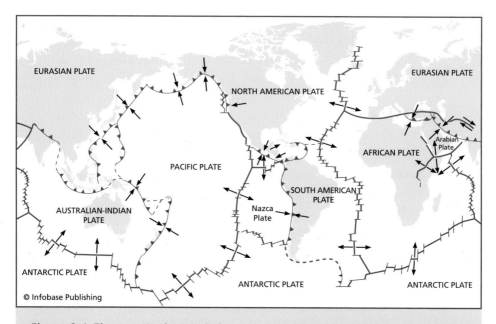

Figure 3.4 *The tectonic plates include seven major plates: the North American plate, the South American plate, the African plate, the Eurasian plate, the Australian-Indian plate, the Pacific plate, and the Antarctic plate.*

slightly offset from each other. Radiating out from between them are what look like stretch marks. The line *between* two ridges is a transform fault. The transform fault is an active margin because the two plates are sliding past each other. The lines that extend beyond the transform fault are not active margins: Both sides of the line are part of the same plate, so there is no relative motion.

Perhaps the most famous transform fault is the San Andreas Fault, which runs through the populated regions of western California. Transform faults are host to frequent earthquakes because built-up stress gets released by a sudden slippage of the two plates. In California, the San Andreas Fault threatens residents of San Francisco, Oakland, and Los Angeles, among other cities. In 1906, an earthquake of magnitude 8.2 devastated San Francisco, spawning fires from ruptured gas lines and killing hundreds of people.

More recently, in 1989, a magnitude 7.1 earthquake collapsed sections of the Bay Bridge and Interstate 280, and killed 62 people throughout the affected area.

THE MAJOR PLATES AND HOT SPOTS

There are seven major plates: the North American plate, the South American plate, the African plate, the Eurasian plate, the Australian-Indian plate, the Pacific plate, and the Antarctic plate (see Figure 3.4). In addition, there are several smaller plates. These include the Arabian plate mentioned previously, and the Nazca plate that is subducting beneath South America to create the Andes Mountains.

The Pacific plate is quickly subducting around much of its perimeter. Recall that subduction zones are often host to volcanoes. Hot magma, generated by the subducting slab, rises up through the overlying plate and erupts at the surface. As a result, the Pacific plate is surrounded by a string of volcanoes known as the "Ring of Fire."

Some volcanoes are not related to active margins. These peculiar specimens sometimes poke up out of the lithosphere for no apparent reason. Known as **hot spots**, they are likely related to a fixed source of hot magma underneath the lithosphere. As the lithosphere moves over the fixed hot spot, the location of the hot spot appears to move.

The Hawaiian Islands are an excellent example of hot spot activity. The Big Island of Hawaii is the youngest and easternmost island. The other Hawaiian Islands are older the further west they are located. In addition to the islands, the chain of volcanoes continues much further to the west and north, but under water. With age, the older volcanoes cooled and submerged below the ocean surface; these submerged volcanoes are called the Emperor Seamounts. The islands and the seamounts were all created by the same hot spot. As the Pacific plate moves west over the fixed hot spot, the hot spot's volcanoes pop up further east on the plate.

CHAPTER 4

Rocks

MOST ROCKS ARE MADE OUT OF MINERALS, WHICH ARE A special kind of crystal. In particular, a **mineral** is any substance with these five properties:

1. Solid
2. Crystalline
3. Natural
4. Inorganic
5. Definite chemical composition

The term "natural" excludes any man-made substance. For example, a crystal grown in a laboratory is *not* a mineral. "Inorganic" means that the substance was not made by a living organism. Since sugar comes from plants, a sugar crystal is *not* a mineral. The phrase "definite chemical composition" guarantees that a mineral has a specific chemical formula, such as NaCl in the case of table salt. In fact, table salt satisfies all five conditions, so it is a mineral.

Scientists have identified over 4,000 different minerals on Earth. Fortunately for students of geology, only a couple dozen are common. Silicates are the most abundant mineral group; by volume, they make up 95% of the Earth's crust. A **silicate** is a mineral made out of silicon and oxygen. The basic building block of silicates is a molecule of silicon and oxygen in the shape of a pyramid. In this pyramid, the silicon atom sits in the middle and the oxygen atoms are at the four corners.

There are as many different silicate minerals as there are ways to connect up the pyramids with each other and with other atoms. In the simplest structure, the pyramid repeats in all directions. Elements like magnesium bond to the oxygen atoms, acting like the glue that holds the pyramids together. The pyramids can also link up with each other by sharing some of their oxygen atoms. They can link up to form single chains, double chains, sheets, and even complex three-dimensional patterns.

WHAT ARE ROCKS?

A **rock** is a natural, solid chunk of minerals, or mineral-like material. Rocks can be composed of a single mineral, a collection of minerals, or a mineral-like substance. An example of a rock that is also a single mineral is a diamond. The second type of rock—a collection of minerals—is simply a mass of individual minerals that are stuck together. These are the most common types of rocks; one example is granite. In some cases, a rock is made out of a mineral-like substance that satisfies most, but not all, of the conditions for being a mineral. One example is pumice, which is quickly dried lava that lacks a crystalline structure. Another example is coal, which is classified as organic because it is made out of ancient plants.

SOLIDIFICATION: FROM MAGMA TO ROCK

Igneous comes from the Latin word "ignis," meaning fire. This is an appropriate name because, as discussed in Chapter 2, igneous rock forms from hot magma. Depending on the chemical composition of the magma and the rate at which it cools, different types of igneous rocks are made. Two main properties of igneous rocks are their texture and their composition.

Ruby, Sapphire, and Emery Boards

When it comes to precious gems, beauty is in the eye of the beholder. Two stones of the same mineral can have very different values depending on how sparkling and transparent they are. Take, for example, the mineral called corundum. *Corundum* is the crystalline form of aluminum oxide, Al_2O_3, and it can have many different appearances, depending on what elements are present in the crystal.

Pure corundum is colorless. If there are other elements present, the mineral can be any one of a variety of colors. Red, transparent corundum is called *ruby*; all other transparent varieties are called *sapphire*. While ruby and sapphire are kept in the jewelry box, one form of corundum gets thrown in the toolbox and the medicine cabinet. *Emery* is a corundum with iron impurities; despite being a close relative of ruby and sapphire, emery is used as an abrasive on sandpaper and emery boards.

Texture

Most igneous rocks are aggregates of minerals. The **texture** of an igneous rock describes the size, shape, and arrangement of those minerals. The most obvious part of a rock's texture is the mineral size. In some rocks, the individual minerals are visible, and in others they are not. The size of the minerals tells you how quickly the rock formed from cooling magma.

If the magma cools slowly, then there is time for the atoms to arrange themselves into large crystals. This produces coarse-grained rocks, which have mineral crystals large enough to see. Coarse-grained rocks form far below the surface, where it takes a long time to cool. An example of a coarse-grained rock is granite.

If, on the other hand, the magma cools very quickly, then the atoms freeze into place faster than they can arrange into large crystals. This produces fine-grained rocks such as **basalt**, in which the minerals are too small to make out with the naked eye. Rocks with a fine-grained texture form near the surface, where the magma can cool quickly.

Composition

As mentioned earlier, silicate minerals make up some 95% of the Earth's crust. Geologists have found it useful to divide silicate minerals and the corresponding igneous rocks into two broad categories: (1) silicates that are rich in iron or magnesium and poor in silicon, and (2) silicates that are rich in silicon and poor in iron and magnesium. Silicates that are rich in iron or magnesium tend to be darker in color than silicates that are rich in silicon. These two classes of silicate rocks can be further classified based on their texture, for a total of four broad categories. Figure 4.1 shows four representative rocks, including the fine-grained and iron-rich basalt, and the coarse-grained and silicon-rich granite. Gabbro is simply the coarse-grained version of basalt, and rhyolite is the fine-grained version of granite.

Granite is a common type of igneous rock made out of many minerals, including the silicon-rich minerals quartz and feldspar. Granite is an intrusive rock, so it has a coarse-grained texture. In other words, individual minerals are clearly visible. Granite is widespread in the continental crust and can be found in many places, including continental mountain ranges, and as a material in kitchen countertops, and your local street-side curb.

Basalt, a common iron-rich rock found in the ocean crust, is an extrusive rock that results from the cooling of magma within the rift valleys of mid-ocean ridges. Because the magma cools very quickly in the ocean, basalt has a fine-grained texture. Compared to granite, basalt is dark and heavy.

WEATHERING: FROM ROCK TO SEDIMENTS

Most of the Earth's surface is covered by small rocks, pebbles, gravel, sand, and soil, not by big slabs of rock. This loose material is made when larger pieces of rock get broken into smaller pieces, a process known as **weathering**. Once weathering has produced smaller rocks

Figure 4.1 *The classification of silicate minerals and rocks is based on content (iron and magnesium versus silicon) and appearance (fine-grained versus coarse-grained). (a) Basalt is a fine-grained mineral with a high iron and magnesium content. (b) Rhyolite is a fine-grained mineral with high silicon content. (c) Gabbro is a coarse-grained mineral with high iron and magnesium content. (d) Granite is a coarse-grained mineral with high silicon content.*

and particles, the loose material can either (1) fall down a slope because of gravity, which geologists call **mass wasting**, or (2) be swept away by wind, water, or ice in a process called **erosion**.

How Do Cracks Form in Solid Rock?

Weathering proceeds more quickly if the rock is already cracked. One way rock can crack is if it gets jolted at a plate margin; earthquakes do this all the time to rocks (and buildings) at the surface. Other cracks are made in more subtle ways.

Figure 4.2 *Devils Postpile in California exhibits columnar jointing that formed as the intrusive igneous rock cooled underground.*

In general, **joints** are defined as cracks that were not created by any movement of the rock. In other words, cracks made by earthquakes are *not* joints. Joints, however, are often made by shrinkage of the rock as it cools. When igneous rock forms from cooling magma, the decrease in temperature can cause the rock to contract and fracture. This is similar to what happens if a hot glass is taken out of the dishwasher and immediately filled with cold water. Many people have learned the hard way that this causes the glass to crack and sometimes shatter. This happens because the cold water quickly cools the glass, causing it to shrink so fast that cracks form.

Some joints form in a regular pattern. Devils Tower in Wyoming and Devils Postpile in California are large igneous rocks that formed intrusively. As the igneous rock cooled, it developed vertical fractures known as columnar joints. As shown in Figure 4.2, the columnar joints created vertical columns of rock that look like gigantic crystals. Like many crystals, the columns also have a regular, often hexagonal cross-section. But they are *not* crystals—they were formed not by chemical arrangement of atoms, but by the shrinkage of the rock as it cooled. Although the rocks and the joints formed underground (intrusively), the surrounding rock was later weathered away. This left the columns of rock rising up above the surrounding landscape.

How Do Rocks Get Weathered?

Most substances expand when heated and shrink when cooled. On the other hand, as water is cooled from 4°C to the freezing point at 0°C, the water *expands* (becomes less dense). When water freezes to ice, it expands even more. This explains why ice cubes float in a glass of water instead of sinking. The lower density of ice, relative to water, also explains why ice forms on the tops of rivers and lakes rather than on the bottom. This behavior of water and ice has an important effect on weathering. As water freezes inside the tiny fractures of rocks, it expands. This expansion puts pressure on the walls of the joint, causing it to widen. This effect plays a dominant role in the weathering of rocks on cold mountain slopes. The result is often a pile of rocks at the base of the slope.

Plant roots are another agent in the physical weathering of rocks. As trees seek water, they send their roots down into fractures in rocks. As the tree grows, so do the roots. The pressure from the growing roots can further open these joints.

Rocks are also weathered by chemical reactions with water. Some minerals, such as table salt, dissolve in water and thus are carried away by rain. Other minerals react with water to make new substances that are less resistant to chemical weathering.

Rain is naturally acidic because of carbon dioxide dissolved in the water. This acidity helps to speed up many of the chemical reactions that break down the minerals in rocks. Air pollution adds even more acidity to the rain, further speeding the chemical weathering. Rain that is more acidic than normal is called acid rain.

What Is Soil and How Does It Erode?

Weathered rock is a major component of soil. **Soil** is a mixture of tiny rock particles, weathered minerals, and organic material from dead plants. Tiny pores in the soil provide space for air and water. For plants, soil is indispensable. Aside from providing a foothold for plants to grow, soil holds on to rain water and supplies much needed nutrients to the plants. Soil also provides habitat for bacteria and fungi, which decompose dead plant material. Together, the soil, plants, fungi, and microorganisms form a complex ecological system.

When it rains, water drops fall on the soil like miniature bombs, dislodging soil particles. Plants protect the soil from this bombardment with their leaves, which act like mini umbrellas. In places where trees have been cut down, this protection is missing and the soil particles are more readily dislodged by the raindrops. As the rain accumulates on the ground, water can begin running downhill and carrying the soil along with it. Plants protect against this erosion with their roots, which act to bind the soil together like stitching. Where the trees have been cut down, however, the roots decompose and are less able to resist the powerful force of the water. Today, much of the Earth's forests have been cut down for wood and to make room for crops. With the protective vegetation gone, the soil is eroding faster than it can be replenished.

LITHIFICATION: FROM SEDIMENTS TO ROCK

The general process of turning sediments into sedimentary rock is called lithification. This process can proceed in two ways: by pressing the sediment together with high pressure or by gluing the sediment together with chemicals that seep into the pore spaces.

Lithification caused by subjecting the sediments to high pressure is called **compaction**. The large pressures are created over millions of years as the layer of sediment becomes buried underneath many layers of other sediments. Compaction works best on sediments with very small particles; as they are put under high pressure, the tiny particles rearrange to eliminate the pore spaces. This process resembles squeezing a sponge, where the air and water is removed from the pores. On the other hand, sediments with large grains, like sand, will not compress much during compaction. This process is more like to trying to compress a bag of marbles.

For the sediments with large grains, the most important type of lithification is **cementation**. In this process, water seeps through the pore spaces of the sediment. Substances that were dissolved in the water come out of solution and collect in between the grains, holding them together like glue. For sediments with small particles, compaction typically leaves little room for water to flow through. As a result, cementation is less effective on fine-particle sediments.

METAMORPHISM: FROM ROCK TO ROCK

Any kind of rock can undergo **metamorphism**, a change in the rock's texture or chemical composition. These changes take place when a rock is heated to high temperatures or is subjected to high pressures, or both. The result is metamorphic rock.

High pressure can change the look of the rock even without the presence of high temperatures. If the pressure is higher in one direction than the others, the pebbles in sedimentary rock can become stretched. Similarly, when an igneous rock experiences higher pressure in one direction, the minerals tend to line up.

Figure 4.3 *Nonuniform pressure can cause the minerals in granite (a) to align in streaks, producing gneiss (b).*

When granite is compressed in this way, the result is the metamorphic rock called gneiss, as shown in Figure 4.3.

A condition of high temperature, but low pressure, can be created if magma enters hollow spaces in the underground rock. As the pool of magma reaches up into the crust, the surrounding rock heats up and begins to alter chemically. This tends to form a rind of metamorphic rock around the edges of the hollow chamber. Most metamorphic rock is produced at convergent plate boundaries where there are both high temperatures and high pressures. As mountains are thrust into the sky, underlying rock is compressed and heated, producing large swaths of metamorphic rock.

MELTING: FROM ROCK TO MAGMA

The final step in the rock cycle is the melting of rock back into magma. This occurs readily at subduction zones, where the slab of oceanic crust plunges into the mantle. As the rock slides into the mantle, temperatures rise to the point where metamorphism takes hold. As the temperatures rise further, the rock begins to melt and becomes magma.

CHAPTER 5

Freshwater

THE FLOW OF WATER AROUND THE EARTH IS A SOLAR-POWERED cycle. As the ocean absorbs sunlight, the energy goes towards evaporating liquid water into water vapor. Although there is a lot of salt dissolved in the ocean water, only the water evaporates off the sea surface, leaving the salt behind. This can be tested at home by leaving a pan of salt water out in the sun for several days. Once all the water has evaporated, the pan will be coated in salt crystals. This is how salt-free water, called **freshwater**, is produced from the salty ocean.

The water vapor evaporated off the ocean can then follow one of many routes in the hydrologic cycle. The vapor will inevitably form clouds that will rain back onto the ocean or out over land. If the clouds rain over the ocean, then the water's journey in the hydrologic cycle is complete—that is, until it evaporates again.

If the clouds rain over land, then the water can take many different paths. The most conspicuous of these paths is the flow of water along the surface from high elevations to low elevations. Since the landmasses sit higher than sea level, water that falls on land flows downslope toward the edges of the continent. Every river in

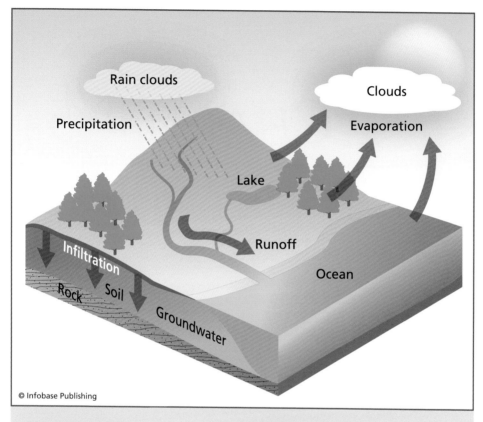

Figure 5.1 *The hydrologic cycle, also called the water cycle, brings water to the continents in the form of rain.*

the world is simply a trail of rainwater trying to make its way back to the ocean. There are other paths in the hydrologic cycle that are available to the water, however, including evaporating off the land surface, being used by plants, or seeping into the ground. All of these possibilities can be traced in Figure 5.1 and will be discussed in the following sections.

WATER VAPOR
Water vapor itself is a colorless gas; it is as invisible as nitrogen, oxygen, and all the other gases that make up the air around us.

Clouds are visible because they are made up of tiny droplets of liquid water. Like little beads of glass, these droplets scatter light and give clouds their white, fluffy appearance.

When the water vapor is too hot or when there is not enough water vapor in the air, water droplets will not form. The reasons for this are fairly straightforward. The formation of water droplets is a balance between two effects: (1) the clumping of water vapor into droplets, and (2) the evaporation of the droplets into water vapor. If the rate of evaporation is faster than the clumping, then droplets cannot form. If the rate of clumping is faster than the evaporation, then droplets will form.

Since liquid water evaporates faster when it is hot, high temperatures guarantee that the would-be droplets evaporate faster than they can form. Low humidity means that the water molecules are spaced far apart, so the droplets cannot form as quickly as they evaporate. When the humidity increases or the temperatures drop, molecules of water vapor can stick together long enough to form droplets. Clouds are most often formed when humid air rises, causing the water vapor in the air to cool.

SURFACE WATER

Any form of water that falls from the sky, including both rain and snow, is called **precipitation**. When precipitation falls on land, it will do one of the following:

- Seep into the ground in a process called **infiltration**.
- Return to the atmosphere by **evapotranspiration**.
- Flow along the surface as **runoff**.

Infiltration is the movement of water down into the ground through soil or porous rock. This water will add to the natural system of groundwater, as we will see later in this chapter.

Precipitation may also evaporate from the soil to return directly to the atmosphere. Plants aid in this process by drawing water up through their roots and releasing it to the air through tiny pores in their leaves. This process is called transpiration. The combined effect of soil evaporation and plant transpiration is called evapotranspiration.

Finally, the water may flow downhill along the land surface as runoff. The water eventually dumps into a channel of flowing water called a stream. In common usage, a stream refers to a small flow of water, somewhere in between a tiny brook and a full-fledged river. To geologists, a **stream** refers to a flow of water of *any* size, so that a babbling brook and a raging river are both considered streams.

STREAMS

Streams can begin wherever rainwater collects on the ground. Small streams gather the runoff from the surface and direct the water into larger streams. It is common for a stream to feed into a larger stream, which then empties into an even larger stream, and so on. This makes for a tree-like branching of streams. Unlike a tree, which continually branches as it grows *upwards*, streams connect up with each other as they flow *downwards*. At the end of the largest streams, the water empties into the ocean or a lake.

Stream Load

With its power to erode sediment, water plays a major role in shaping the Earth's surface. Over time, the net effect of a stream is to transport sediment downstream, from a higher elevation at its beginning to a lower elevation at its end. All of the sediment carried by the stream is referred to as the stream's **load**.

A stream's load can be divided into three categories:

1. The *suspended* load consists of the particles suspended in the water.
2. The *bed* load counts all the larger particles that are bounced, dragged, and rolled along the bottom of the stream.
3. The *dissolved* load is all the material dissolved in the water.

Typically, the suspended load makes up the largest part of all sediment carried by the stream. The suspended load consists of particles small enough to be kept aloft in the swirling water. The maximum size of the suspended particles increases as the discharge of the stream increases. In other words, a slow stream can only keep small particles suspended. If the stream speeds up, it will pick up larger particles from the bottom and keep them suspended in the water. This also works in reverse. If the stream slows down, the larger particles settle out of suspension and get deposited on the bottom. This fact plays an important role in the shaping of streams, as we will see shortly.

The bottom of a stream is called the bed. The bed load consists of particles and rocks too large to be kept aloft in the water, but that are light enough to be moved along the bottom. These particles can slide or roll along the stream bed. Some particles also move by a kind of leaping motion that occurs when swirling currents briefly kick the particle aloft.

The dissolved load consists of substances dissolved in the water. Usually, the dissolved load is a small fraction of the stream's total load. The dissolved load is largest when groundwater, often high in dissolved material, feeds into the stream.

Stream Dynamics

When water drops some of its load, this is called **deposition**. The deposition of suspended sediments onto the stream bed has the opposite effect of erosion. When the route of erosion equals the route of deposition, the stream is in equilibrium. In this case, the depth of the bed does not change because the material that is washed off the bed is replaced with new sediments.

When erosion is greater than deposition, the stream actively deepens its valley. The stream's suspended load acts like a sandblaster, grinding away at the rock on the stream floor. Just as a carpenter could cut through a plank of solid wood by sanding one spot for many hours, a stream can cut its way through solid rock by eroding it over many thousands of years. An example of such a stream is shown in Figure 5.2a.

If deposition is greater than erosion, then the stream channel can become choked with sediment. As a stream slows down, the largest particles in the suspended load begin to settle out on the bottom. As these sand-sized particles accumulate, they can form

Figure 5.2 *(a) Erosion, shown in Horseshoe Bend in the Colorado River, can deepen a stream's valley by removing large amounts of rock over time. (b) Resurrection River, near the town of Seward, Alaska, is an example of a braided stream, which results when deposition of sediment outpaces erosion.*

a mound of sand. If this mound becomes too big, the stream will be forced to go around it, sometimes splitting into two streams to go around the mound on either side. As sand accumulates in these new paths, the stream may split again. The result, shown in Figure 5.2b, is called a *braided* stream because the network of streams resembles braids.

Even in streams that are not choked with sediment, there is a tendency for the stream to develop large bends called **meanders**. Water does not travel with the same speed everywhere in a stream—the fastest currents are near the outside of a turn, like race cars hugging the outside of a turn on a race track. Since the faster currents have a greater capacity to erode, the outside bank erodes as the stream cuts into it. This tends to make the bend larger, creating meanders.

Meanwhile, the slowest currents are near the inside edge of the meander. Recall that faster currents can carry more suspended load than slow currents. As the water slows down going around the inside edge of the bend, it deposits some of its suspended load. These deposits accumulate to make a mound of sediment on the inside edge of a meander.

If the meanders get too big, then adjacent sections of the stream may meet up as depicted in Figure 5.3. Given a choice, streams prefer to flow through the shorter of two paths, so the water chooses the route through the new channel, or cutoff. What remains from the neglected meander is a crescent-shaped lake.

We have discussed how streams carry loads of sediment and how these loads play a role in shaping the course of a stream. But where does all the sediment eventually end up? Much of the sediment will accumulate at the end of the stream. At the stream's end, the water suddenly enters a larger pool of water, either a larger stream, a lake, or the ocean. When the stream water flows into this larger space, it slows down. This causes much of its load to be deposited.

When the stream empties into the ocean, the deposits form a **delta**. Famous examples include the Nile Delta and the Mississippi Delta. The city of New Orleans is built on the Mississippi Delta. Much of the city is at or below sea level, which makes it very susceptible to flooding. When Hurricane Katrina hit New Orleans in

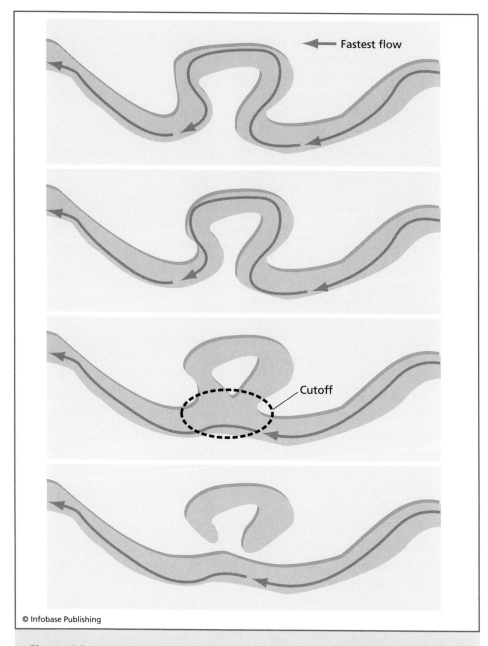

Figure 5.3 *As a meander grows, the region of fast flow breaks through to produce a cutoff, shortening the length of stream.*

Prospecting for Gold

*W*hen a stream flows around a turn, the flow rate decreases on the inside bend. This causes the larger and heavier particles in the load to be deposited. If the stream is carrying gold or diamond from eroded rock near the head of the stream, then these heavy pieces are likely to be deposited in the inside bend. These accumulations of valuable metals and minerals are called placer deposits.

In early 1848, gold placer deposits were discovered at Sutter's Mill on the American River in California. By the end of the year, a full-fledged gold rush was underway, with people flocking to the area in hopes of making their fortune. The discovery of gold changed the history of California and the nation.

2005, large parts of the city were flooded and destroyed when the levees built to protect the city from floodwaters broke, and almost 2,000 people lost their lives.

GROUNDWATER

Massive volumes of water exist below the ground. In fact, the volume of water under the ground is many times larger than the volume of all the lakes and rivers. This **groundwater** moves through the tiny pores and cracks within the soil and rock. Although this water moves very slowly, typically a few meters a day or even only a few meters per year, the groundwater *does* flow. Groundwater is fed by infiltration of water from the surface. This water eventually flows out of the ground into streams and lakes.

For the most part, this entire process takes place well out of sight. Perhaps the most obvious sign of groundwater activity is the delayed response of runoff to a downpour of rain. If there were no infiltration and no groundwater system, then rain would flow off the surface of the land almost as quickly as it arrived. But this does

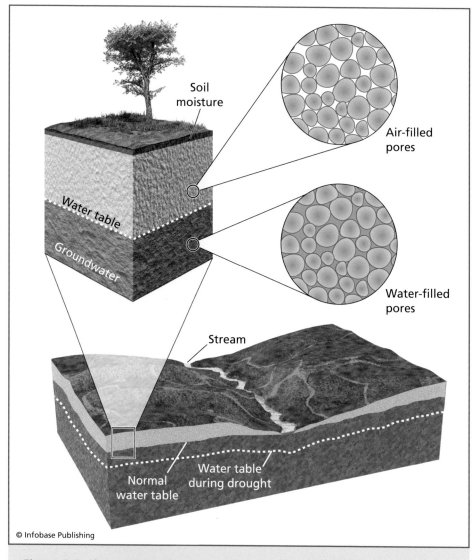

Figure 5.4 *After a rainfall, the water table slowly discharges the extra groundwater into streams.*

not happen. Instead, streams continue to flow long after the rain has stopped. This occurs because much of the precipitation has seeped into the groundwater, which continues to feed the streams.

Groundwater Basics

Rock is not as solid as it looks. As noted previously, within all rock formations are cracks and tiny holes that can hold water. Within the loose sediment and soil that overlie the rock, the spaces between grains also allow passage for water. The greater the volume of these openings, the more water the rock or sediment can hold. The more interconnected the openings, the more easily the water can flow from place to place.

As water infiltrates into the ground after a rainfall, it first encounters rock and sediment that have air-filled holes. The water can readily pass through these open spaces until it reaches further down where the spaces are already filled with water. The surface that separates the air-filled and water-filled regions is called the **water table**, which is depicted in Figure 5.4. Once the rainwater has reached the water table, it cannot move any further down because the spaces in the sediment and rock are already occupied by water. Instead, the rainwater fills the holes and spaces directly above, causing the water table to rise.

Just like water on the surface, groundwater flows from high levels to low levels. Immediately after rainfall, the water table matches up with the contours of the land. As the groundwater flows downward, the water table flattens out, sending water from high points to low points. The net effect is to discharge groundwater into streams that touch the water table.

Groundwater Effects

Most underground caves are created by the action of groundwater. As water flows through certain types of rock, such as limestone, the water can carry away some of the rock in solution. As the water dissolves away the rock, it can create vast networks of caves. The larger the caves become, the less structural support there is for the overlying rock and sediment. If a cavern becomes too large, it may collapse. At the surface, this forms a **sinkhole**, a large depression in the land. Where many underground caves have been made by groundwater, the surface may be dotted with sinkholes.

When the groundwater seeps out of the rock on the ceiling of a cave, some of the chemicals can precipitate out of solution onto the ceiling. Over time, these deposits grow into long, conical shapes called stalactites. Once the drop falls to the ground, more of its dissolved chemicals will precipitate onto the floor of the cave. If the drops continue to fall from the same spot on the ceiling, then long, conical shapes called stalagmites will form on the ground. One way to remember the difference between these two types of deposits is to think of the "c" in stalactite as standing for "ceiling" and the "g" in stalagmite as standing for "ground."

CHAPTER 6

Historical Geology

THE EARTH'S HISTORY IS A LONG AND FASCINATING TALE. To make sense of it all, we must have some kind of time line. In the study of modern history, time is given as the number of years since a specific date. The year "zero" was chosen to be a time about 2,000 years ago. In this system, the number of years increases with time.

Unlike most people, geologists count time backwards. They refer to an event in Earth's history as taking place a certain number of years before *now*. One reason why geologists count time backwards is that there is no well-defined starting point in Earth's history. The two logical events to choose would be the Big Bang or the formation of the Earth. Unfortunately, neither of these dates is known with any great precision. In addition, even if scientists knew that the Earth was formed exactly 4,651,391,532 years ago, it would be cumbersome to refer to 7,000 years ago as the year 4,651,384,532. For these reasons, geologists date events in Earth's history by the number of years before the present. Some abbreviations are commonly used, such as "kya" for thousands (<u>k</u>ilo) of <u>y</u>ears <u>a</u>go and "mya" for <u>m</u>illions of <u>y</u>ears <u>a</u>go.

Geologists use a variety of techniques to peg a date to an event in the geologic record. This event might be the formation of a rock or the death of a particular animal. Types of dating that produce a numerical year—the number of years before present—are known as *numerical dating* (or *absolute dating*) methods. Before the technology for numerical dating became available in the twentieth century, geologists had to rely exclusively on the method of *relative dating.* This method uses rock and sediment layers to put geologic events in order. Despite the advances in numerical dating, relative dating is still a very important technique.

RELATIVE DATING METHODS

A **stratum** is a distinct layer of sediments or sedimentary rock. Several layers are referred to as *strata.* Strata can be seen in many places, including along the banks of an ancient river, along the side of the highway, in a pit dug into the soil, and in a cliff by the sea. Look back at Figure 5.2a, which shows strata exposed at a stream valley. Most people do not stop to look at these layers, but they hold a great deal of information for a geologist.

Relative dating uses strata to put different events in order from oldest to youngest. Unlike numerical dating, which requires expensive machinery, relative dating requires only simple logic. For example, the principle of **superposition** states that, given one stratum on top of the other, the lower layer is older. When geologists talk about the age of a stratum, they are referring to how long ago those sediments were deposited. The principle of superposition is just common sense: As sediments gather on the ground, each layer accumulates on top of layers that were deposited earlier. Despite its simplicity, superposition is a very powerful idea. For example, a visitor to the Grand Canyon might wonder which layers of the canyon walls are oldest and which are the youngest. If the visitor understood the principle of superposition, he or she would be able to automatically order all the layers, from the oldest on the bottom to the youngest on the top.

Although this principle works well on a single cliff wall, it does not tell us how to compare two different layers from two different locations. For example, if a geologist were studying a stratum in New Jersey and another stratum in Spain, how would he or she figure out which is older? To compare layers from different sites, a geologist must study the properties of those layers. Some of the most useful clues within sedimentary layers are the fossils they contain.

Over hundreds of millions of years, plants and animals have evolved through different stages. Some fossils are unique to their particular stage in Earth's history. Dinosaur fossils come from a time called the Mesozoic. An extinct group of marine arthropods called trilobites come from an earlier time called the Paleozoic. These facts can be used to order strata from different places. If the layer in New Jersey contains trilobites and the layer in Spain contains dinosaur bones, then the New Jersey layer is older than the layer in Spain.

NUMERICAL DATING METHODS

As discussed in Chapter 2, some isotopes are stable and others are radioactive. For geologists, a useful law of physics states that radioactive isotopes decay at a constant rate. Since radioactive decay takes place in the nucleus, it is not affected by chemical interactions: An atom will decay at the same rate no matter where it is. This fact means that radioactive isotopes make excellent clocks.

An isotope's decay rate is measured as a **half-life**. The half-life is often written as τ, the Greek letter tau. The half-life is the amount of time it takes for half of the atoms to decay. In one half-life, an atom has a 50-50 chance of decaying. These atoms are the perfect version of a coin toss. Given a single radioactive atom, there is a 50% chance that it will be unchanged after time τ and a 50% chance that it will have decayed into a different isotope.

Imagine a pile of 1,000 atoms, all of the same radioactive isotope. Each one has a 50% chance of surviving the first length of time τ. On average, about half will survive, leaving 500 of the original atoms. After waiting an additional time τ, another half will have decayed, leaving only 250 atoms. After three half-lives, about 125 will remain, and so on. A plot of this process for carbon-14, which has a half-life of 5,730 years, is given in Figure 6.1.

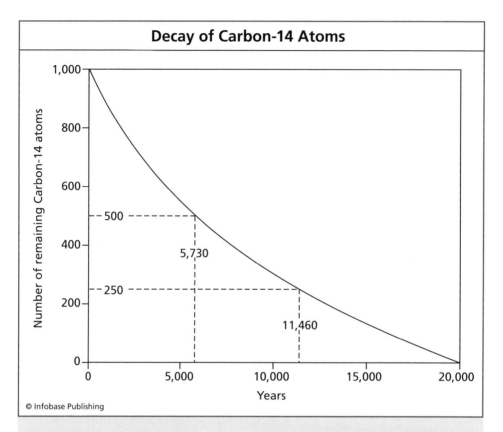

Figure 6.1 *The half-life of carbon-14. The number of atoms that remain decreases by a factor of two every 5,730 years.*

Working backwards, you can calculate how much time has elapsed from the number of isotopes that remain. For example, if half of the radioactive atoms are left, then one half-life has elapsed. If only $\frac{1}{16}$ of the atoms remain, then four half-lives have elapsed ($\frac{1}{2} \times \frac{1}{2} \times \frac{1}{2} \times \frac{1}{2} = \frac{1}{16}$).

Scientists can measure how long ago a plant or animal died using a method called **radiocarbon dating**. The word *radiocarbon* refers to the radioactive carbon isotope, ^{14}C, or carbon-14. The most common form of carbon is ^{12}C, which has 6 protons and 6 neutrons, for a total of 12 nuclear particles. Carbon-12 is a stable isotope of carbon. The carbon-14 isotope also has 6 protons (otherwise, it would not be a carbon atom), but it has 8 neutrons, giving it a total of 14. Carbon-14 decays to the stable isotope of nitrogen by emitting an electron, which turns one of its neutrons into a proton: $^{14}C \rightarrow {}^{14}N$ + electron.

Carbon-14 has a half-life of 5,730 years, so it is most useful in dating plant and animal remains that were buried within tens of thousands of years ago. The original abundance of ^{14}C in living tissue is fixed by the constant bombardment of particles in the upper atmosphere. Cosmic radiation, the flux of charged particles that hits the Earth from outer space, converts nitrogen in the atmosphere into radiocarbon. The ^{14}N atom absorbs a neutron and spits out a proton, turning a nucleus with 7 protons and 7 neutrons into a nucleus with 6 protons and 8 neutrons, which is ^{14}C.

Cosmic radiation ensures that there is a constant ratio of ^{14}C to ^{12}C in the atmosphere. When plants consume carbon dioxide from the air, the new plant life contains carbon with the same ratio of ^{14}C to ^{12}C. When animals eat the carbon-filled plants, they also acquire the same fraction of radiocarbon.

Since this book is made out of trees, it also has the same ratio of carbon-14 to carbon-12 as the atmosphere. Over time, however, the carbon-14 in this book will decay. A scientist who finds this book thousands of years from now will be able to date it by measuring the amount of carbon-14 (or by reading the date on the copyright page).

THE EARTH'S HISTORY

The Earth's calendar is called the **geologic time scale**. Like an ordinary calendar, the geologic time scale has several divisions of time. From longest to shortest, these divisions are called eons, eras, periods, and epochs. Few people can actually recite the names of all the epochs, but all geologists must at least know the eons and eras. The geologic time scale is displayed in Figure 6.2, where time increases from the formation of the Earth at the bottom to the present day at the top.

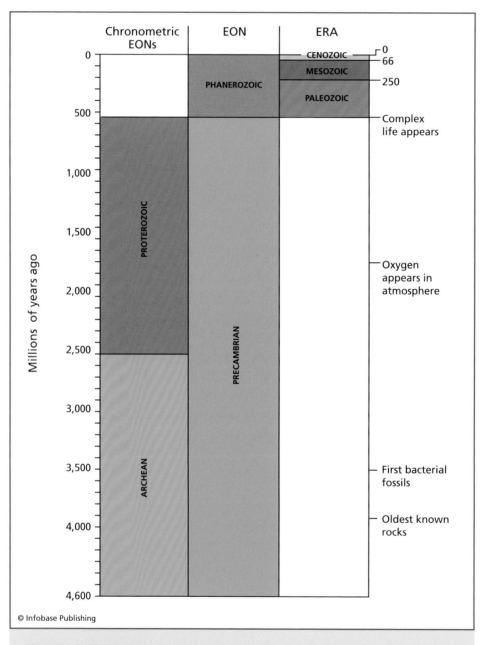

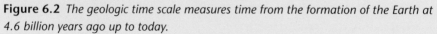

Figure 6.2 *The geologic time scale measures time from the formation of the Earth at 4.6 billion years ago up to today.*

There are a few different versions of the geologic time scale, and the beginning and ending dates for the divisions are frequently revised. Some people use a system with three or four eons, but the simplest version has only two: the Precambrian and Phanerozoic. The **Precambrian** eon begins at the formation of the Earth and ends 540 million years ago.

During the Precambrian, there was no life on land, because plants and animals had not yet evolved to live there. Although the continents were lifeless, the oceans teemed with some of the first life forms—a kind of bacteria called *blue-green algae*. These microorganisms may have been small, but, as we will see shortly, they had a big impact on the early atmosphere.

In the early Precambrian, the atmosphere contained no oxygen. Today, atmospheric oxygen allows animals to breathe and it filters out 99% of the sun's ultraviolet rays. Without a protective blanket of oxygen, plants and animals on land would be scorched by the sunlight. Fortunately, blue-green algae helped to generate oxygen through the process of photosynthesis.

Photosynthesis is the method by which plants and algae generate their own mass and provide their own energy. Powered by sunlight, photosynthesis converts water (H_2O) and carbon dioxide (CO_2) into carbohydrates (CH_2O) and oxygen (O_2):

$$\text{Energy from sunlight} + H_2O + CO_2 \rightarrow CH_2O + O_2$$

A fortunate byproduct of this reaction is oxygen, which plants and algae exhale to the surrounding waters and the atmosphere. During the Precambrian, the blue-green algae photosynthesized carbon dioxide into oxygen. As dead algae sank to the bottom of the ocean, their carbon collected on the sea floor while oxygen accumulated in the atmosphere.

Thanks in part to the work of the blue-green algae, oxygen-breathing life began to flourish at the beginning of the **Phanerozoic** eon. The word Phanerozoic, meaning "visible life," refers to the sudden abundance of complex life that appeared in fossils after 540 mya. Because the Phanerozoic is such an important time in

Earth's history, scientists have divided this eon into three eras: the *Paleozoic* (meaning "ancient life"), the *Mesozoic* (meaning "middle life"), and the *Cenozoic* (meaning "recent life").

The Paleozoic stretches from 540 mya to 250 mya, and it encompasses a fantastic time in Earth's history. Evolution produced an ocean that was teeming with exotic creatures, including an abundance of trilobites. During the Paleozoic, many species of plants and animals evolved to live on land. The Mesozoic is sometimes known as the Age of the Dinosaurs. The Mesozoic, however, witnessed not just the rise of the dinosaurs, but also the appearance of mammals, birds, and flowering plants. At the end of the Mesozoic, about 66 mya, the dinosaurs suddenly went extinct. Many scientists believe that this extinction was caused by the collision of a large meteorite with Earth. Whatever the cause, the extinction of the dinosaurs opened the way for mammals, including eventually humans, to flourish during the Cenozoic.

Each of the eras is divided into periods, which are, in turn, divided into epochs. The human species evolved during the **Pleistocene** epoch, which began about 1.8 million years ago and ended 10,000 years ago. Human civilization developed since the end of the Pleistocene in the current epoch known as the **Holocene**. The Pleistocene and Holocene are so short compared to the rest of Earth's history that it is not possible to print these subdivisions within the Cenozoic era in Figure 6.2.

THE ICE AGE

The Pleistocene is often called the Ice Age because it was a time of frequent cold temperatures. During this epoch, the Earth cycled between cold periods called **glacials** and warm periods called **interglacials**. The cold glacials usually took about 90,000 years and the warm interglacials lasted roughly 10,000 years. The glacials and interglacials alternated back and forth with almost clockwork regularity. Figure 6.3 shows a plot of global temperature during one of these cycles.

The total cycle—glacial plus interglacial—takes about 100,000 years, so it has repeated itself ten times in the past million years.

The current epoch, the Holocene, is simply the most recent interglacial. Scientists do not yet know why the glacials come and go in a 100,000-year cycle, and it is unclear how long the current interglacial will last.

Because the cycles have been so regular, many scientists suspect that small, predictable changes in Earth's orbit are responsible. As the Earth orbits the sun, the gravitational pull of the other planets causes Earth's orbit to wobble. These cyclic changes in Earth's orbit cause slight changes in the amount of sunlight that the Earth receives.

According to the **Milankovitch theory**, a reduction of sunlight results in a glacial (cold period) and an increase in sunlight causes an interglacial (warm period). The orbital variations have cycles that repeat every 20,000 years, 40,000 years, and every

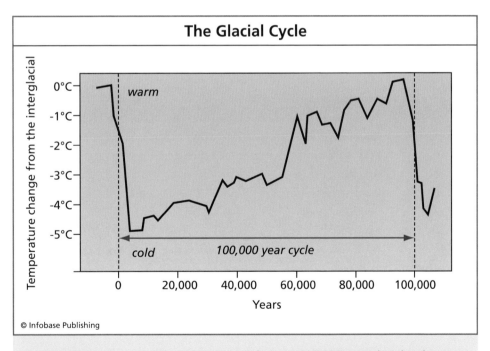

Figure 6.3 *A graph of global temperatures during a 100,000-year glacial cycle.*

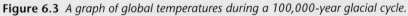

100,000 years. Unfortunately, the 20,000- and 40,000-year Milankovitch cycles are much stronger than the 100,000-year Milankovitch cycle. Because of this fact, the Milankovitch theory has a hard time explaining why the Ice Age cycles should be 100,000 years long rather than 20,000 or 40,000.

While the physics of these Pleistocene cycles is not well understood, the history has been well documented. The best-documented glacial was the most recent one that terminated between 20,000 and 10,000 years ago. During the last glacial, large amounts of snow accumulated in northern America and northern Europe. Gradually, the snow became compact and hardened into ice. Towards the end of the glacial, Canada and parts of the northern United States were smothered in a blanket of ice several kilometers thick. On the island of Manhattan, the ice sheet was taller than the Empire State Building.

Instead of sitting still, the ice sheet slowly slid towards its southern boundary, where its edge melted into the sea. As it moved south, it ground away at the bedrock and transported boulders many hundreds of kilometers. The oddly placed boulders and rocks that can be found scattered throughout New England are the result of this process. The many lakes of Canada, and even the Great Lakes themselves, were carved out of the Earth by the ice.

Conditions during the last glacial are so different from our everyday experience that they can be difficult to imagine. Yet the modern world *does* contain regions that are gripped in ice: Antarctica, Greenland, and many high mountains. The large, grinding chunks of ice in these parts are called glaciers, and they are the topic of the next chapter.

CHAPTER 7

Glaciers

MOST PEOPLE WHO LIVE IN TEMPERATE REGIONS OF THE world, including the United States and Europe, are quite familiar with snow. During a snowstorm, the flakes accumulate into a fluffy layer that blankets just about everything. Over days and weeks, the snow slowly disappears by a combination of evaporating directly into water vapor and, if temperatures are above freezing, by melting into water. By the time the warmer temperatures of spring take hold, the snow has melted away.

Air is colder at higher altitudes in the atmosphere. Up in the high mountains, it is so cold year round that the snow does not melt even over the summer. At these high altitudes, the snow on the ground is perennial—it lasts all year long.

Temperatures cold enough for perennial snow may also be found near the poles of the Earth. **Latitude** is a measure of the distance from the equator, increasing from 0 at the equator to 90 degrees at each of the poles. At higher latitudes, closer to the North or South Poles, temperatures are colder. This results from the angle at which the sun's rays hit the Earth. Near the equator, the sun's rays hit the Earth perpendicular to the surface. Like a flashlight pointed directly at the wall, the light is bright and intense at the equator. At higher latitudes, the sun's rays strike the surface at a glancing angle. Tilting the same flashlight to produce a long streak of light on the wall, the amount of light per area decreases. Similarly, the higher latitudes of Earth receive less sunlight per unit area than do the lower latitudes; the result is colder temperatures near the poles.

In the polar regions of the Earth, perennial snow is common. Of course, the snow cannot be accumulating endlessly—if it did, the oceans would dry up and all the water in the world would end up as snow and ice near the poles. Each grain of snow and ice *does* eventually leave the polar regions. In fact, the amount of perennial ice in the polar regions is roughly constant: Ice is added at the same rate that other ice melts away. Ice is usually added as snow in the cold region (high altitudes and high latitudes). The ice then flows at a snail's pace towards the warmer region (lower altitudes and lower latitudes), where it melts away. These massive bodies of ice on land, gradually moving downhill under their own weight, are called glaciers. Processes related to glaciers are often referred to as **glacial**. (This adjective is not to be confused with glacial the noun, which is a name for the cold periods during the Ice Age.)

TYPES OF GLACIERS

Glaciers exist in several varieties, from patches of ice in the mountains to large swaths of ice covering entire continents. Not all bodies of ice are glaciers. To be a glacier, the ice must be on land, it must be perennial, and it must move under its own weight. The sea ice that covers the North Pole is not a glacier because it floats entirely on water. The foot of snow that fell in the backyard last winter does not qualify as a glacier: It does not survive the summer and, while the melted water may flow, the ice itself does not.

One of the smallest types of glaciers is a **cirque glacier**, as pictured in Figure 7.1a. This glacier lives in a bowl-shaped basin, called a cirque, that is created by the glacier as it erodes the mountain. Today, many mountains have empty cirques near their peaks.

These are where cirque glaciers carved out a home during past glacial periods. Unlike larger mountain glaciers, cirque glaciers do not extend far below their basin.

Valley glaciers, on the other hand, begin in a cirque and extend down the mountain through a valley. These valley glaciers carry sediment down and off the mountain. From the air, these bands of sediment are clearly visible in the ice. Valley glaciers are also known as mountain or alpine glaciers.

In regions with high precipitation and cold temperatures, glaciers may become the dominant surface feature. Currently, these conditions are met in Greenland and Antarctica, which exist at or near the two poles. Both Greenland and Antarctica are almost entirely covered with ice that is several kilometers thick. These continent-sized glaciers are called **ice sheets**.

GLACIER DYNAMICS

When snow falls, it forms a fluffy layer on the ground, 90% of which is air. This low density results from the fact that intricate snowflakes cannot pack tightly together. Over time, the density can increase as water evaporates off the edges of the snowflakes and solidifies onto the center of the flakes. This makes the grains of snow more compact, which allows them to be packed closer together. This dense and hard form of snow is an intermediate between fresh snow and solid ice. Over several years, the weight of overlying snow forces out the remaining air; this produces solid ice.

Usually a glacier flows so slowly that the motion is not visible. Some of the first observations of glacial flow were performed by laying down rocks on the surface of the glacier; upon returning many months later, the rocks had moved downstream. Typical flow rates are between a few centimeters per day to a few meters per day. Perhaps the most amazing thing is that the ice flows at all. Everyday experience tells us that ice is a brittle solid—it will shatter if hit hard enough, but it will not bend. Only underneath 50 meters (164 feet) of ice is the pressure great enough for ice to bend instead of breaking.

Under the force of gravity, glacial ice moves downhill through two processes. If the bottom of the glacier is frozen to the bedrock, then the glacier can only move by bending. If the glacier is not frozen to the bedrock, then the glacier may also slide along the ground. In general, a combination of these two types of motions contributes to glacial flow.

For every glacier, there is a region uphill where ice accumulates and a region downhill where ice melts away. In the **ablation area**, ice melts faster than the rate of snowfall. This region is on the lower part of the glacier where temperatures are warmer. As the ice melts, a stream may form that carries the water away. If the glacier ends in a lake or the ocean, large sections of ice may split off and float away as icebergs, a process called calving. Ablation refers to all processes of ice removal, including melting and calving. If the glacier is in equilibrium, then the rate of ablation *from* the ablation area is exactly matched by the sum of snowfall and ice flow *into* the ablation area.

In the **accumulation area**, the snowfall is greater than the loss of ice from melting. Here, fresh snow is added and the deeper layers of snow slowly convert into ice. If the glacier is in equilibrium, then the rate of snowfall *into* the accumulation area is exactly matched by the sum of ablation and ice flow *out of* the accumulation area. The line separating the accumulation area and ablation area is called the **equilibrium line**. At this line, snowfall equals ablation.

GLACIAL EROSION

Much like a stream abrades and erodes the surrounding material, a glacier grinds away at the surrounding rock as it flows. The resulting debris freezes into the glacial ice and becomes known as **till**.

In Figure 7.1b, the valley glacier is streaked with lines along the direction of flow. These dark lines are accumulations of till called **moraines**. The term moraine also applies to the mounds of till deposited on land by the glacier. As a valley glacier flows, the sides of the glacier grind rocks of all sizes off the valley walls. This forms moraines along the sides of the glacier known as *lateral* moraines.

Figure 7.1 *(a) A cirque glacier does not extend much beyond the bowl-shaped cirque in which it grows. (b) Medial moraines are clearly visible in this valley glacier.*

When two valley glaciers converge, their lateral moraines merge into a single moraine running down the middle of the combined glacier. These moraines, known as *medial* moraines, are clearly visible in Figure 7.1b. Following the right medial moraine back up the valley, one can see where it formed from convergence of two lateral moraines.

As a glacier melts at the bottom edge of the ablation area, the till that is too large to be carried away by the meltwater is left behind. If a glacier exists for a while at equilibrium—neither advancing nor retreating—then a *terminal* moraine will accumulate in an outline of the glacier. Some terminal moraines are rather small, while others, such as those created by ice sheets, can be the size of entire cities.

THE WISCONSIN GLACIAL

As discussed in Chapter 6, each glacial/interglacial cycle lasts about 100,000 years. The glacial, or cold period, takes up most of that time. The interglacial, or warm period, is relatively short in comparison. The Holocene epoch coincides with the current interglacial that has extended from roughly 10,000 years ago until the present. Before the Holocene, the *Wisconsin glacial* gripped much of North America, Europe, and Asia in cold temperatures. Ice sheets, like the ones that cover modern-day Greenland and Antarctica, spread out over much of North America and Europe, destroying everything in their path.

The ice sheet that covered North America during the Wisconsin glacial is called the *Laurentide ice sheet*. At its center in Canada, the Laurentide ice sheet measured 3,000 meters (about 2 miles) thick. Like all glaciers, the ice sheet grew by the accumulation of snow at high latitudes (northern Canada) and high altitudes (the mountains). As it gathered mass, the ice spread down into the mountain valleys and connected up with other valley glaciers. Eventually, a single ice sheet formed out of the many valley glaciers.

When a glacier grows to the size of an ice sheet, it starts to affect the weather. The large volume of ice can actually deflect the global air currents. In addition, glaciers are white, so they reflect sunlight extremely well. Anyone who has spent time outdoors in the snow on a sunny day can recall how long it takes for their eyes to adjust when they return indoors. By reflecting the sunlight, an ice sheet cools the surrounding air and allows for its continued growth. The Laurentide ice sheet cooled its surroundings enough to grow over most of Canada and the northern United States.

As a glacial progresses, the ice sheets grow larger, reflect more sunlight, and cool the entire Earth. This process continues until the ice sheets reach their largest extent and the Earth reaches its coldest temperatures at a time called the *glacial maximum*. The glacial maximum during the Wisconsin, called the *Last Glacial Maximum (LGM)*, occurred approximately 20,000 years ago. At that time, the locations of modern-day Chicago, Boston, and New

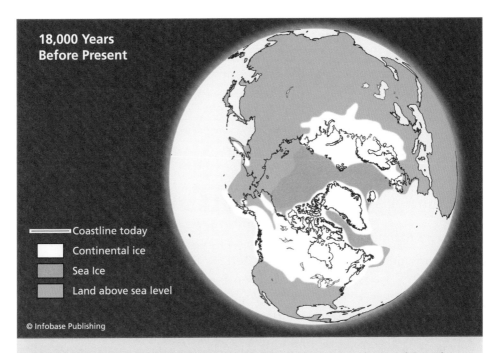

Figure 7.2 *At its greatest extent, the Laurentide ice sheet covered most of Canada and much of the northern United States, including the locations of modern-day Boston, New York, and Chicago.*

York were buried underneath the gigantic Laurentide ice sheet. The area covered by the Laurentide ice sheet during the LGM is mapped out in Figure 7.2.

By the beginning of the Holocene interglacial, the Laurentide ice sheet had all but disappeared. In its wake, it left many telltale signs of its awesome power. Through abrasion, an ice sheet scrapes the ground as it slowly grinds its way from the high, northern regions towards the coastal margins of the continent. Glacial abrasion removes the topsoil and much of the weaker rock. Where an ice sheet scrapes along bedrock, long, parallel grooves known as **striations** may be cut into the hard rock. Such striations are visible in bedrock in many parts of the northern United States, including exposed bedrock in Manhattan's Central Park.

By plucking away chunks of rock, a glacier can loosen, detach, and transport very large boulders. Plucking begins when water

Figure 7.3 *Three glacial erratics, boulders displaced by a moving glacier, are found on Spitsbergen Island in Spitsbergen, Norway.*

Satellite Imagery of the Canadian Lakes

The many lakes of Canada were created by the erosive action of ice sheets during the Pleistocene. Using maps.google.com, click on the Hybrid button and zoom in to just about any part of Canada to see the many lakes that dot the surface. This patchwork of poorly drained lakes is called *deranged.*

Panning over to Quebec (the province directly above Vermont, New Hampshire, and Maine), look for an almost perfectly circular lake. This circular feature was *not* created by glaciers, but by a meteorite impact 212 million years ago. The lake is dammed along the river that stretches directly south from the reservoir, right where Route 389 crosses it. If you have difficulty finding the dam, type in "50.647N, 68.725W." For more information, Google "Reservoir Manicouagan."

underneath the glacier penetrates cracks in the bedrock. As the water freezes, the cracks widen in the process of weathering discussed in Chapter 4. Once loosened, large chunks of rock rip off the bedrock and freeze into the glacier.

Unlike a stream of water, ice can hold enormous chunks of rock for as long as the ice stays frozen. In this way, the Laurentide ice sheet transported boulders hundreds and thousands of kilometers before dropping them in places far from their origin. Such boulders can be found throughout the northern United States, often sitting conspicuously in the middle of a flat field. An example is shown in Figure 7.3. These rocks are called **erratics** because they do not resemble the bedrock in the area in which they were dropped.

Among the most noticeable legacies of the Pleistocene Ice Age are the many lakes that the ice sheets left in their wake. Where an ice sheet moved over a pocket of soft rock, plucking and abrasion created depressions in the Earth's surface. And where glacial till accumulated in valleys, old stream paths became clogged. Both of these effects helped to form the many lakes that dot the surface of Canada. In some cases, the lakes created by the ice sheets are gigantic: The Great Lakes were created in a complicated glacial process near the boundary of the Laurentide ice sheet.

The ice sheets affect not only the land, but also the ocean. During a glacial, large quantities of water accumulate on land in the form of ice. As the ice sheets grow, more and more water is taken out of the ocean and stored on the continents. During the Last Glacial Maximum, so much ice had accumulated on land that the ocean level had dropped by 100 meters (328 feet). This lowering of the sea level exposed land that is usually inundated with water during an interglacial. For example, a land bridge connected Britain and France where the English Channel exists today. A land bridge also connected Alaska to Russia where today the Bering Strait separates the two. The Bering land bridge allowed the ancestors of Native Americans to migrate into North America from Asia many thousands of years ago.

CHAPTER 8

Wind

Tʜᴇ ᴍᴏᴠᴇᴍᴇɴᴛ ᴏꜰ ᴛʜᴇ ᴀɪʀ ɪꜱ ᴘᴏᴡᴇʀᴇᴅ ʙʏ ᴛʜᴇ ꜱᴜɴ. Aꜱ sunlight heats the Earth's surface, hot air rises up and pulls air along the ground to take its place. These winds have their greatest effect in barren deserts, where high winds can erode rock and shape the sand into giant mounds known as **dunes**.

THE ATMOSPHERE

The atmosphere can be divided into several layers. The **troposphere** extends from the ground to about 11 kilometers (6.8 miles); it is the region where all weather occurs. By volume, the troposphere is the smallest of the various layers, but it still contains most of the atmosphere's air. This is possible because, although the other layers have more volume, the air in them is far less dense.

As a rough rule, the density of air decreases by one half for every 5 kilometers (3.1 miles) of altitude. This halving rule is similar to the half-life decay of radioactive isotopes. In this case, the "half-distance" is 5 kilometers (3.1 miles). Therefore, the air at the top of Mount Everest, which is at an altitude of 8.85 kilometers (about 5.5 miles), is only about 1/3 as dense as the air at sea level. Since density is mass per volume, a climber's lungs at the top of the mountain will contain only one-third the amount of oxygen as they would at sea-level. This explains why most climbers have to use oxygen tanks to make the ascent up Mount Everest.

The other atmospheric layers are the stratosphere, mesosphere, thermosphere, and exosphere. The **stratosphere** contains molecules of ozone, O_3, that absorb ultraviolet (UV) radiation. This ozone helps protect life on the planet's surface, including humans, from harmful radiation.

Movements of air within the troposphere are powered by the sun. As the sun warms the ground, the air nearest the ground heats up and expands. This expansion makes the air lighter and, just like a hot-air balloon, the air rises. As the air cools by radiating its heat out to space, the air becomes denser and sinks back to the ground.

This cycle of rising and sinking air produces wind. On small scales—the size of cities and towns—the winds can be very fickle. The winds may blow from the east one moment, blow from the west the next, and then stop altogether. These fluctuations of winds are very chaotic, which is what makes the local weather so difficult to predict. But on very large scales—such as the size of continents—the prevailing winds follow a predictable pattern called the **atmospheric circulation** (Figure 8.1).

ATMOSPHERIC CIRCULATION

Recall from Chapter 7 that more sunlight is received near the equator than at higher latitudes. The intense sunlight causes air at the equator to expand, rise, and spread out towards higher latitudes. As this air cools, it descends towards the ground near 30 degrees latitude in both the Northern and Southern Hemispheres. This cool air then travels along the ground back towards the equator. This cycle of air is known as the **Hadley cell**. There are two Hadley cells: one operating between the equator (0°) and 30°N, and the other between 0° and 30°S. Both Hadley cells can be seen just above and below the equator in Figure 8.1.

In the language of weather, the direction of a wind is specified by the direction from which it comes, not by where it is going.

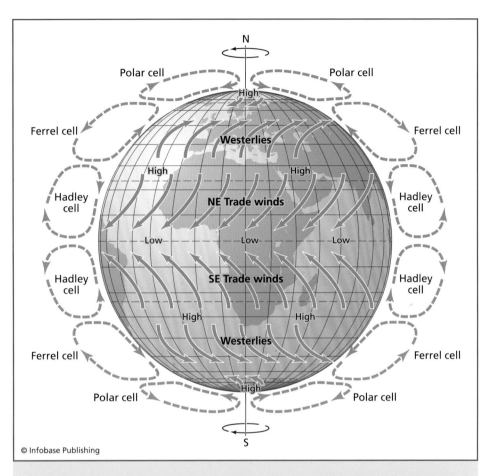

Figure 8.1 *Atmospheric circulation is dominated by the Hadley, Ferrel, and polar cells.*

This means that a *north wind* is a wind that flows from the north to the south. An *east wind* blows from the east towards the west. Likewise, *west winds* and *south winds* are winds that blow towards the east and north, respectively.

Since humans live on the surface of the Earth, the winds that most people care about are those that move along the ground. For people who live in the tropics, the ground winds they experience are generated by the Hadley cell as the air flows back towards the equator. If there were nothing more to the story of the Hadley cell, then people living between the equator and 30°N would experience a north wind and people living between the equator and 30°S would experience a south wind. But because the Earth rotates, these winds do not travel directly north or south. Through a phenomenon called the **Coriolis effect**, all winds tend to be deflected to the right in the Northern Hemisphere and to the left in the Southern Hemisphere.

The Coriolis effect results from the fact that different latitudes of the Earth move at different speeds. This fact may seem counterintuitive, but it is actually very simple. Picture a spinning merry-go-round: A person sitting at the outer edge of the merry-go-round moves quickly in a large circle while a person near the center travels slowly in a small circle. Likewise, the equator of the Earth travels the fastest, moving towards the east at about 1,670 kilometers per hour, or 1,040 mph. At higher latitudes, the speed of the Earth's surface is slower; at the poles, like at the center of

Flushing Bad Science

The Coriolis force is a very real phenomenon. Not only does it affect the large-scale movements of the atmosphere, but it also affects weather systems. Hurricanes, for example, are a low-pressure system; as the air gets sucked in towards the low-pressure center, the winds get deflected by the Coriolis force. In the Northern Hemisphere, this causes all hurricanes to rotate counter-clockwise. In the Southern Hemisphere, hurricanes rotate clockwise.

It is often taught that the Coriolis force is responsible for the way water spins as it drains down the sink or gets flushed down the toilet. This is not true. The Coriolis force is very small, so a system has to be very large (like a hurricane) to be appreciably affected by it. Water draining down a sink swirls as it drains because of asymmetries in the basin; water flows down a toilet in whatever direction the water jets are oriented.

a merry-go-round, the only motion is a slow rotation—one 360° turn every 24 hours.

As an air mass moves towards the equator, the ground underneath it moves faster and faster towards the east. To observers on the ground, this makes the air look as if it is getting deflected to the west. In the other direction, air moving away from the equator gets deflected to the east. In the Northern Hemisphere, this means that air gets deflected to the right, and, in the Southern Hemisphere, air is deflected to the left.

Because of the Coriolis effect, the air in the Hadley cell gets deflected towards the west as it flows towards the equator. These east winds are called **trade winds** because of their historical importance to trade when ships relied on sails for power. The Coriolis effect is also responsible for the fact that storm systems spin counterclockwise in the Northern Hemisphere. In large storms, the air gets sucked along the ground towards the low-pressure center. The air gets deflected to the right by the Coriolis effect, causing the air to spin counterclockwise. In the Southern Hemisphere, the air spins clockwise because the air moving towards the low-pressure center gets deflected to the left.

The **polar cells** operate in much the same was as the Hadley cells. Warm air rises at about 60° latitude and sinks at the poles. Along the ground, the air moves away from the poles and so it gets deflected to the west, just like the trade winds. These surface winds are referred to as the *polar easterlies*.

In between 30° and 60° latitude, a different kind of atmospheric circulation dominates. Here, the **Ferrel cell** causes air to *sink* at 30° and *rise* at 60°. As a result, the surface air moves northward and is deflected by the Coriolis effect towards the east. These westerlies are responsible for the general movement of storms from west to east across the United States.

WIND EROSION

As seen in Chapter 5, water is responsible for a great deal of erosion. While wind is not as powerful an eroding agent as water, the wind can move particles much like a stream does. Particles can move in the wind by being held aloft in the air or by being kicked along the ground by gusts. Like a stream, the amount and sizes of particles that are transported by the wind depend on the wind's speed. If the wind picks up speed over dry and dusty ground, additional particles will be picked up and carried aloft. If the wind slows down, the larger particles will fall out of the air and be deposited on the ground.

The wind has its greatest impact on dry regions that lack vegetation. Where the ground is moist, the particles of sediment are held together by water and are difficult for the wind to pry apart. Where there is vegetation, the plants shield the ground from the strongest winds and their roots hold the sediments in place. Only in desert-like areas, with little water or plants, do winds have a major impact on the landscape.

Wind erodes the land through two processes, deflation and abrasion. In the process called deflation, the wind simply picks up loose material and carries it away. In abrasion, wind-borne particles collide with objects on the surface, slowly grinding them away.

Since smaller particles are more easily carried aloft than larger particles, deflation tends to carry away the fine sediment while leaving behind the larger stones. As the fine grains blow away, the larger stones are left behind. After a long time, these stones form a layer called a *desert pavement* that shields the sediment below it from further deflation.

Abrasion can wear away one side of a rock as the wind-borne particles continually pock tiny holes in the surface facing the wind. This sandblaster effect is analogous to how a stream erodes solid rock with its suspended load. In the desert, the abraded surfaces of rocks indicate the direction of the winds.

WIND-BLOWN FORMATIONS

Something interesting occurs when an object, such as a large rock, blocks the path of the wind. In the shielded space directly behind the rock, the air slows down. Since sediment is dropped by the wind when its speed decreases, deposits accumulate behind the obstacle. This phenomenon is familiar to those who live in snowy parts of the country. In a windy snowstorm, deposits of snow will accumulate to the downwind side of a parked car.

In deserts, the winds can pile up mounds of sand known as dunes. Most dunes have an asymmetrical cross-section in which one side is more gently sloped than the other. The gentle slope faces the wind; the steeper slope is on the downwind side of the dune. Dunes come in a variety of shapes. In regions with a limited supply of sand, winds tend to form crescent-shaped dunes. The two horns of these crescent-shaped dunes point downwind. When there is more sand at the surface, steady winds will form wave-like ridges of sand aligned perpendicular to the direction of the wind.

CHAPTER 9

The Shoreline

THE SHORELINE IS THE NARROW BOUNDARY BETWEEN THE land and the ocean. While it occupies only a small fraction of the Earth, the shoreline is an important site of erosion. Since coastal regions are also home to millions of people and thousands of ports, the natural erosion that takes place there can have significant consequences.

SOURCES OF WAVE ENERGY

For the most part, the shoreline is shaped by the wave energy of the ocean. Energy is carried through the ocean in the form of waves, and these waves derive their energy from three different sources. These three sources are wind, the gravitational pull of the moon, and seismic activity.

Wind Energy

The most common waves—such as those that continuously crash on the beach—are formed by the wind. As the wind passes over the surface of the ocean, areas of high air pressure push the sea

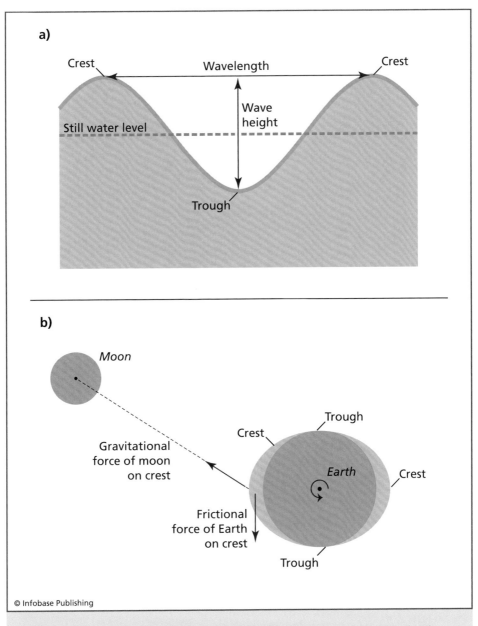

Figure 9.1 *(a) Waves are characterized by alternating crests and troughs. (b) The gravitational pull of the moon makes two crests that try to stay aligned with the moon as the Earth spins.*

surface down and areas of low air pressure pull the sea surface up. This produces the typical wave pattern of crests and troughs shown in Figure 9.1a. Since the winds are produced by solar heating of the atmosphere, it is correct to say that the ocean's waves derive their energy from the sun.

Tidal Energy

While wind is the dominant source of wave energy in the ocean, it is not the only source. Tidal waves are produced by the gravitational interaction between the Earth and the moon. Every year, the Earth imparts some of its rotational energy to the moon. As a result, the Earth's rotational speed slowly decreases and the moon moves away from the Earth by about 3.8 centimeters (1.5 inches) per year. The slower the Earth rotates, the longer it takes for a day to pass. About 900 million years ago, the Earth spun much faster than today: The length of a day was only 18 hours. Since that time, the tidal interaction between the Earth and the moon has lengthened a day to 24 hours.

Not all of the Earth's rotational energy gets transferred to the moon. In fact, most of the energy goes into the ocean in the form of tides. To someone sitting on a beach, the tides look like an overall rise and fall in the level of the ocean that repeats twice a day. Measured from space, these tidal waves look like an elliptical bulge that is straining to align with the direction of the moon despite the fact that the Earth is rotating beneath it (see Figure 9.1b). Since the moon moves very little in 24 hours, a point on the surface of the Earth will pass through two crests (two high tides) and two troughs (two low tides) in the course of one day.

Seismic Energy

Every so often, a disturbance underneath the sea will create a huge wave known by its Japanese name, **tsunami** (pronounced "soo NAH mee"). These waves are sometimes called *tidal waves*, but this name is a misnomer because tsunamis have nothing to do with the tides. Instead, tsunamis are created by **seismic** (earthquake) activity, or by another underwater event such as a volcanic eruption or a landslide.

Where the ocean floor moves upward, a bulge on the ocean surface will develop. Similarly, a downwards movement of the seafloor will create a depression in the ocean surface. Either way, a wave is created that travels away from the site of the earthquake. Out in the open ocean, the tsunami wave is rather mild. The wave may rise roughly a meter above normal sea level and have a length of hundreds of kilometers. Once the wave enters the shallow waters near the shore, however, the wave will get taller and narrower, rising as high as 30 meters (100 feet).

PHYSICS OF WAVES

A wave has alternating crests and troughs. The distance between two adjacent crests is the **wavelength**. The wavelength is also equal to the distance between adjacent troughs. The vertical distance from trough to crest is the **wave height**.

A wave is a moving disturbance of the ocean's surface. Although the wave may move at a constant speed, the water molecules do not

The Indian Ocean Tsunami of 2004

On December 26, 2004, an earthquake struck a subduction zone in the Indian Ocean. A 1,200-kilometer (746-mile) stretch of seafloor slipped some 15 meters (50 feet) over the course of a couple minutes, creating a powerful tsunami. This wave propagated across the Indian Ocean and grew to be over 20 meters (66 feet) high in spots where the wave broke on land. The effect of the tsunami was devastating, destroying shoreline communities and killing over 200,000 people.

Much of this loss of life could have been avoided if there had been a way to detect the tsunami and warn the millions of people living in the Indian Ocean area. A timely warning would have allowed people to move away from the coast to higher ground. In response to the tragedy of 2004, the United Nations has called on the international community to establish a global tsunami detection and warning system.

travel along with the wave; the water molecules move in a circular fashion underneath the wave. This circular motion may be observed by watching an object floating on the surface as the wave passes. At the beach, the gentle waves beyond the breakers do not carry the bubbles, seaweed, or swimmers to the shore. Instead, all the floating objects (including people) simply move up and down in a small circle as the wave passes by.

As a wave approaches shallow water, its wavelength decreases and its wave height increases. This effect is familiar to anyone who has spent time watching the waves at the beach. The incoming waves begin as broad, low swells that gradually grow taller and narrower as they move towards the shoreline. Once the wave becomes too tall, the crest topples over and the water molecules *do* begin traveling along with the frothy wave, carrying sand and body surfers along with them.

SHORELINE FEATURES

As discussed in Chapter 7, the sea level has been rising ever since the beginning of the current interglacial. Over the past 18,000 years, melting of the ice sheets has caused the sea level to rise about 120 meters (400 feet). Rising sea levels initiated rapid erosion of many coastal regions, a process that continues today.

A common shoreline feature is the **sea cliff**. Waves carry their energy on the surface of the water; as these waves pound on the edge of a cliff, they erode it from the bottom. This leaves a steep, sometimes overhanging cliff that is vulnerable to mass wasting. Eventually, the overhanging ledge collapses, but the waves will continue to cut into the cliff in a continual cycle of erosion and mass wasting.

Since the wave action only cuts horizontally into the land, a surface of rock and debris may be left just at or below sea level. The larger this **wave-cut platform** becomes, the longer the waves have to travel over it before they reach the cliff. As they travel over the platform, the waves dissipate some of their energy and are then less effective at eroding the sea cliff.

Where there is a **headland**—a stretch of land that juts out into the ocean—the ocean can shape fantastic structures by erosion.

When a wave hits a headland, it will tend to bend so as to wrap around it. The bending of the waves is caused by the fact that waves travel more slowly in the shallow water surrounding the headland—this causes waves to bend towards the shallower water. The net effect is to focus much of the wave energy on the headland.

As the waves pound the sides of the headland, *sea caves* may be carved out of the rock. As the caves grow, they may erode all the way through the rock to form a *sea arch*. Subject to further erosion, the sea arch will eventually collapse, leaving an isolated mass of rock just off the shore known as a *sea stack*. These structures are depicted in Figure 9.2.

When waves strike the shore at an angle, large quantities of sand can be moved along the beach. This **longshore drift** occurs because the waves push sand up the beach at an angle when the

Figure 9.2 *Shoreline features include a wave-cut platform and headland showing a sea cave, sea arch, and sea stack.*

waves crash on shore. When the water recedes back down the beach, it does so directly back into the ocean. This causes sand to follow a zigzag path up the beach: up and to the side when the wave crashes on the beach at an angle, then directly down when the water recedes, and then repeated for each successive wave. When taking a dip in the ocean where longshore drift is present, bathers will recognize that the water tends to drag them parallel to the shore and away from their beach blankets.

Longshore drift can transport large quantities of sand. Sometimes, the drift will carry and deposit sand past a corner in the natural shoreline. When this happens, a sand bar can develop that effectively continues the beach in the direction of the drift. This strip of sand is called a spit. As longshore drift continues to operate up the side of the spit, additional sand gets deposited at the tip of the spit, causing it to grow.

Spits can sometimes grow so large that they surround an entire bay and seal off the former shoreline. Even larger structures, such as **barrier islands**, can form by the elongation of spits. Not all barrier islands are created this way, however. Some barriers are created by the deposition of sand by storm waves, and others may be remnants of former sand dunes that have been submerged by the rising sea.

Barrier islands are common features along the Gulf and Atlantic coasts of the United States. Increasingly, they have also become popular vacation destinations. Of course, building a home on a sand bar is not always a wise decision. When a violent storm passes through, the waves can wash away the sand and the homes built on top of it. This fact is rediscovered every time a major hurricane strikes a populated stretch of barrier islands.

CHAPTER 10

Humans

Throughout Earth's history, various organisms have played a major role in shaping the Earth, especially its climate and land surface. We noted how, during the Precambrian, blue-green algae helped convert the atmosphere's carbon dioxide to oxygen. During the Paleozoic, various types of plants evolved to live on land. These pioneering plants transformed Earth's barren landscape into a blanket of green.

Today, one organism—the human species—is transforming the planet at a record pace. Humans have spread out over every inhabitable part of the globe, transforming the land and altering the climate. Some of the effects of human civilization are easily visible from an airplane window: cropland, pasture, and urban development now cover much of the world. Other effects are less visible but no less important. As humans continue to burn coal, oil, and natural gas for energy, some of the atmosphere's oxygen is being converted back to carbon dioxide. With a population of more than 6 billion, the human species is now one of the major forces shaping the Earth.

LAND USE

Humans have substantially altered the land by cutting down or burning the natural vegetation and replacing it with crops, pasture, and pavement. Cropland now covers about 10% of the land surface. These intensively cultivated plots have replaced natural forests and grasslands, and have displaced many of the animals that once lived there. While crops supply grains, vegetables, and fruit, pasture is used to feed animals, such as cows, for the production of meat and dairy products. Lands used for pasture now cover about 20% of the land surface. Cropland and pastures have been established on much of the Earth's fertile ground.

Buildings and pavement have also claimed a large portion of the Earth's surface: Around 3% of the Earth is used directly for humans' living space. As people in industrialized countries have moved to the less densely populated suburbs, the area of cities has grown much faster than the population of cities. This spreading of urban areas into the surrounding land is called **urban sprawl**. This sprawling expanse of cities and towns requires a vast network of roads, which, in turn, cause fragmentation of the landscape by dissecting patches of land into smaller and smaller pieces. Animals that once roamed freely now find themselves trapped within smaller patches of land by the highways and roads that surround them.

Land use is the major contributing factor to the problem of extinction. While extinction of species is a natural part of evolution, the pace of extinction is now 100 to 1,000 times higher than the natural rate in the past. In only the past 2,000 years—a blip of time in geologic terms—humans have driven one-quarter of all bird species to extinction, and many others are endangered.

Humans affect not just the vegetation and animals that live on the land, but also the basic geologic cycles that act on the land. Recall that the hydrologic cycle brings water to the continents in the form of rain. That rain recharges the groundwater, nourishes plants, and runs towards the ocean in streams (see Figure 5.1). Today, however, humans divert about half of the runoff within streams, 70% of which goes to irrigate crops. In the United States, 98% of rivers have some of their water diverted for human uses.

In the case of some of the world's largest rivers, so much water is withdrawn that very little of it reaches the ocean.

Groundwater also supplies a great deal of water for human use. In many places, the groundwater is being extracted faster than it can be recharged by precipitation. This results in a lowering of the water table, leaving less water for use in the upcoming decades. In some places, the groundwater is recharged only very slowly. For example, most of the groundwater underneath the sands of Saudi Arabia is thousands of years old. Yet Saudi Arabia uses this groundwater for most of its water needs, which is a clearly unsustainable practice. A similar situation exists in the Midwestern United States, where groundwater is pumped for irrigation at a much faster rate than it can replenish.

In addition to altering the flow of water, human activities have also changed the chemical composition of lakes and rivers. Through the use of fertilizers, laundry detergents, and the release of sewage, freshwater and coastal marine waters contain more nutrients than they would naturally. This may sound like a good thing—after all, nutrients are supposed to be good for you. But, as with all things in life, too much of a good thing can cause trouble. This is especially true of the extra nitrogen and phosphorous that now pollute the water in many places.

Nitrogen and phosphorous are important nutrients that plants and animals need to survive. To help their crops and lawns to grow, humans sprinkle these fields with fertilizers that contain these nutrients. The nitrogen and phosphorous from the fields eventually get washed into streams, into lakes, and out to sea when the rain falls. This causes the water to be too high in nutrients, a condition known as **eutrophication**. The high level of nutrients causes microscopic algae to grow out of control, turning the water brown, green, or red. Some of these algae are toxic, but all types of algae—if present in sufficient numbers—can kill fish by using up oxygen in the water. The thick clouds of algae can also block out the light that the plants in the water use for photosynthesis. As the plants die, the fish that rely on them as a source of food suffer as well.

Another source of excess nutrients is sewage, especially when it is released into the water without proper treatment. During the middle to late part of the twentieth century, laundry detergent also contributed to the problem because manufacturers added phosphorous to their products to make clothes feel softer. In the United States, detergent manufacturers ended this practice voluntarily in 1994.

Other types of chemicals are released to streams and groundwater from mining activities. Mining now causes more material to be moved than the natural process of erosion discussed in Chapter 5. In the United States, about 8,000 kilograms (18,000 pounds) of stone and gravel *per person* are moved every year. When this rock gets disturbed by mining, much of it gets exposed to the weathering effects of air and water. If the newly exposed rock contains sulfur compounds, the sulfur can combine with oxygen to produce sulfuric acid. As water flows through the rock, this acid

Satellite Imagery of Land Use

One way to appreciate the impact that humans have had on the land's surface is to survey the Earth with satellites. Using maps.google.com, click on the Satellite button, zoom in to a random part of the United States, and look for signs of human activity. Land use by humans shows up as unnatural-looking shapes: rectangular plots of cropland, straight stretches of road, and the familiar shapes of buildings.

In fact, the United States is so developed that it is more difficult to find a patch of land that has *not* been altered by mankind. For comparison, pan down to the Amazon, which is the vast green part of northern South America. Zooming in to the center of this green patch, it is possible to find patches that have no obvious human influence. However, the Amazon is quickly being lost to the timber industry and the clearing of trees for crops and pasture; these disturbances show up as patches of light green and brown, usually near roads and rivers.

can be carried into nearby streams and groundwater, in a process called **acid mine drainage**.

In the western United States alone, between 20,000 and 50,000 mines are generating acid and polluting streams. In addition to the acid, toxic metals are also dissolved out of the rock and into the food chain. Some of these metals can end up in the food that humans eat, causing a variety of illnesses.

GLOBAL WARMING

Most of the environmental problems discussed so far are local effects that result from local actions. For example, clearing a plot of land affects mainly the plants and animals that live on that land. Polluting the groundwater or digging a mine pit affects the local area and has little effect on the plants, animals, or humans living halfway around the world. But some pollutants that get emitted locally end up having global consequences. One such pollutant is carbon dioxide gas, or CO_2.

As noted in Chapter 2, carbon dioxide makes up less than 0.1% of the atmosphere. CO_2 is a nontoxic gas. In fact, every time an animal or person exhales, they emit carbon dioxide. It is also essential for the growth of plants, which use it as a source of food. And yet, as we have seen in the case of eutrophication, too much of a good thing can cause severe problems.

Carbon dioxide is a **greenhouse gas**, which means that it traps heat. The warming of the Earth's atmosphere that results from greenhouse gases is called the **greenhouse effect**. Although the term greenhouse effect comes from an analogy with greenhouses used for growing plants, the analogy is technically incorrect. In a greenhouse, sunlight enters through the glass and warms up the ground, which, in turn, heats the air. The hot air is buoyant and wants to float into the sky to be replaced by cool air from above. In a greenhouse, the hot air is trapped and prevented from mixing with cooler air outside the greenhouse. A similar effect occurs when a parked car is left out in the sun with the windows rolled up. In contrast, the so-called greenhouse effect in the atmosphere does not prevent the rising and mixing of hot air—hot air rises just fine with or without greenhouse gases. Instead, the greenhouse gases slow down the rate at which energy gets returned to space as a kind of invisible light called **infrared radiation**.

Light is a type of wave, and like waves on an ocean, it comes in many different wavelengths. The human eye can only see light that has a wavelength in a narrow range called the **visible spectrum**. Different colors correspond to different wavelengths in that range: Blue has the shortest wavelength in the visible spectrum and red has the longest. Infrared radiation is light whose wavelength is longer than red light, so it cannot be seen by the human eye. Although we cannot see infrared light, it is emitted by every object with a nonzero absolute temperature. Everything that contains heat slowly radiates its energy away as infrared radiation, and the Earth is no exception. The Earth loses energy to space as infrared radiation at the same rate that it receives energy from the sun. This is why the Earth stays a relatively constant temperature despite absorbing a constant flux of sunlight.

Recall that the Earth receives, on average, 342 watts per square meter (W/m^2) of sunlight energy. All of this energy eventually radiates back out to space, but the energy can follow many different paths to get there. Only a small amount (67 W/m^2) of the total incoming sunlight gets absorbed by the atmosphere. This is because the incoming sunlight is concentrated in the visible spectrum and greenhouse gases do not absorb visible light. Once the visible light is absorbed by the ground, however, it can only be re-emitted as infrared radiation. This infrared radiation gets absorbed by the greenhouse gases and re-emitted by the gases back towards the surface, which is how greenhouse gases "trap" heat from the sun. The higher the concentration of greenhouse gases, the more infrared radiation gets returned to the Earth's surface, making it warmer.

In general, the greenhouse effect is a good thing. Without it, the Earth would be unbearably cold. But if there is too much greenhouse gas, the planet will get unbearably hot. Of the several types of greenhouse gases, carbon dioxide (CO_2) is the most troubling because it has a very potent greenhouse effect and its concentration has been increasing rapidly. The CO_2 added to the atmosphere in the past 200 years has caused the planet to get warmer. This ongoing increase in the Earth's temperature, primarily caused by the emission of carbon dioxide, is called **global warming**.

Not all emissions of carbon dioxide contribute to global warming. To understand why requires an understanding of the carbon cycle. For the most part, plants are made out of carbon, oxygen, and hydrogen. As noted in Chapter 6, during photosynthesis, a plant uses the energy of the sun to combine water from the soil and carbon dioxide from the air to make carbohydrates:

$$\text{Energy (sunlight)} + H_2O \text{ (water)} + CO_2 \text{ (air)} \rightarrow$$
$$CH_2O \text{ (plant)} + O_2 \text{ (air)}$$

A byproduct of this process is oxygen (O_2), which gets released to the atmosphere. The carbon, on the other hand, gets taken out of the atmosphere and locked up in the tissues of the plant.

When an animal eats a plant, the carbon and hydrogen are "burned" with oxygen to provide a source of energy:

$$CH_2O \text{ (plant)} + O_2 \text{ (inhaled air)} \rightarrow CO_2 \text{ (exhaled air)} +$$
$$H_2O \text{ (urine, sweat, exhaled water vapor)} + \text{Energy}$$

This respiration returns the carbon to the atmosphere. Even if the plant does not get eaten, it will eventually die and be decomposed by bacteria that also exhale the carbon as CO_2. In general, this biological cycle does not change the amount of carbon dioxide in the air: Every atom of carbon taken up by plants eventually gets returned to the air. Over geologic times, slight imbalances in this cycle can change the amount of carbon dioxide in the atmosphere. An imbalance can occur if plant material gets buried before it can be eaten or decomposed. This will cause the amount of carbon dioxide in the atmosphere to decrease as it gets stored underground.

Just like animals, which need oxygen to breathe, bacteria need oxygen to decompose plant material. In places where the water contains very little oxygen, dead plants and algae can be buried with little decomposition. Where this occurs in swampy areas on land, plant tissue can be transformed into coal. In the sea, near the coast, algae can collect on the ocean floor and eventually become deposits of oil and natural gas. Today, many deposits of oil are found on land that was once covered over by ocean water.

Since the beginning of the industrial era in the 1800s, the **fossil fuels** of coal, oil, and natural gas have been widely burned as a source of energy. Coal is a black rock burned in power plants to generate electricity. Oil is a black liquid used to make gasoline, diesel fuel, jet fuel, heating oil, plastics, and other petroleum products. Natural gas is a colorless gas used to heat homes, cook food, and, increasingly, to generate electricity. All three are primarily made out of carbon.

As these fossil fuels are burned, the carbon that has been locked underground for millions of years gets released to the atmosphere as carbon dioxide. About half of the CO_2 is absorbed by the oceans, but the other half is accumulating in the air. In the 1700s, the amount of carbon dioxide in the atmosphere was 0.027%. Today, Earth's air contains 0.038% carbon dioxide, which is a 40% increase.

As the amount of atmospheric carbon dioxide has increased, so has the Earth's temperature. Since 1750, the average global temperature has increased 0.8°C (about 1.4°F). Although that may not sound like very much, it is useful to note that the average temperature difference between a glacial and an interglacial is only 5°C. Even more worrisome are the projected temperature increases projected to occur if countries do not begin to curb their emissions of carbon dioxide.

Some scientists prefer to refer to global warming as **climate change** in order to emphasize that, along with the temperature increase, other aspects of the climate are changing as well. Some parts of the world will get much warmer than other parts, and patterns of precipitation and storm activity will change as well. To date, the northern parts of Canada and Russia have seen the largest amount of warming, and most of that extra warmth occurs during the winter. This has caused extensive melting of glaciers, frozen soil, and the North Pole ice cap.

If the burning of fossil fuels continues unchecked, the impacts of climate change will be widespread. Already, glaciers are retreating worldwide, and many will have disappeared entirely by the end of the century. In the United States, all of the glaciers in Glacier National Park will likely disappear by the year 2030.

Also of concern are the ice caps of Greenland and West Antarctica. A complete melting of the Greenland ice sheet would raise sea level by 7 meters (30 feet), and if the West Antarctic ice sheet collapsed, sea level would rise an additional 5 meters (16 feet). A sea level rise of only a few meters would flood coastal cities around the world, including New York City and much of the state of Florida.

In addition to the rising temperatures and rising sea levels, the pattern of precipitation is also projected to change. Areas that now receive plentiful rainfall may end up receiving little rain in the new climate. In many parts of the world, crops that once flourished may have to be abandoned when precipitation decreases.

Perhaps the most serious concerns are those changes to Earth's climate that cannot be predicted. By studying the history embedded in ancient rocks and glaciers, geologists have learned that the climate can change in sudden and unpredictable ways. Scientists now know that the Earth has certain thresholds beyond which the climate system responds in dramatic ways. In some cases, the entire global climate has been rearranged in as little time as one decade. Scientists do not yet know if the current global warming is pushing the Earth towards such a threshold. Global warming is, perhaps, the single largest environmental challenge faced by humanity. If left unchecked, it will have serious consequences for the entire Earth.

GLOSSARY

ABLATION AREA The region of a glacier where the snowfall is less than the loss of ice from melting and calving.

ACCUMULATION AREA The region of a glacier where the snowfall is greater than the loss of ice from melting and calving.

ACID MINE DRAINAGE The production of acidic water as a result of groundwater or rain water flowing through a mine or a pile of mine waste.

ASTHENOSPHERE The solid, yet malleable, layer of rock that allows the hard lithosphere to "float" upon it.

ATMOSPHERIC CIRCULATION The predictable, large-scale movement of winds over the Earth, dominated by the Hadley, Ferrel, and polar cells.

ATOMIC NUMBER The number of protons in an atom.

BARRIER ISLAND A long island of sand that runs parallel to the shore.

BASALT A type of dark, fine-grained, extrusive igneous rock that is rich in iron and magnesium and poor in silicon. Basalt is very common in the ocean crust.

BIG BANG The explosion that formed the universe about 13 billion years ago.

CATASTROPHISM The incorrect theory that all of the Earth's features were formed in catastrophic events, like Noah's flood.

CEMENTATION A type of lithification in which the grains of sediment are hardened together by chemical processes.

CIRQUE GLACIER A small glacier that sits in a bowl-shaped basin of a mountain and does not extend down into the valley.

CLIMATE CHANGE The current changing of the Earth's climate, caused by an increase of greenhouse gases in the atmosphere, especially carbon dioxide.

COLLISION ZONE A convergent margin in which pieces of continental crust collide with each other.

COMPACTION The forcing together of particles, reducing the empty space in between. For sediments with small particles, this is an important step in lithification.

CONTINENTAL DRIFT The movement of the continents in relation to one another.

CONVECTION   The transfer of heat generated by the rising of hot, light matter and the sinking of cool, heavy matter.

CONVERGENT MARGIN   A margin between two plates that are moving towards each other.

CORE   The ball of iron with a 2,900 (1,800 mile)-kilometer radius that sits at the center of the Earth.

CORIOLIS EFFECT   The deflection of air currents to the right in the Northern Hemisphere and to the left in the Southern Hemisphere, caused by the Earth's rotation.

CRUST   The thin (8- to 70-kilometer [5- to 43.5-mile]) layer of silicate rock that sits on top of the mantle.

DELTA   An accumulation of sediment in a lake or the ocean at the mouth of a stream.

DEPOSITION   The laying down of sediments. Also known as sedimentation.

DIVERGENT MARGIN   A margin between two plates that are moving away from each other. New crust is generated here by the cooling of magma.

DUNE   A mound of sand deposited by the wind.

EQUILIBRIUM LINE   The boundary between accumulation and ablation areas of a glacier.

EROSION   The removal of rock and soil by wind, water, or ice.

ERRATIC   A glacially deposited rock or boulder that is different from the bedrock of the area.

EUTROPHICATION   A condition in which the levels of nutrients in the water are too high, often causing algal blooms.

EVAPOTRANSPIRATION   The combined effect of evaporation from the ground and transpiration from plants.

EXTRUSIVE   The term used to describe igneous rock that cooled from lava above the Earth's surface.

FERREL CELL   The circulation of air that sinks at 30 degrees latitude and rises at 60 degrees latitude.

FOSSIL FUELS   The remains of ancient plants and animals that are burned for energy—coal, oil, and natural gas.

FRESHWATER   Water with very little salt in it, such as the water found in lakes and streams.

GEOLOGIC TIME SCALE   The Earth's calendar, which is divided into eons, eras, periods, and epochs.

GEOLOGY   The study of the Earth.

GEOTHERMAL   Pertaining to heat from within the Earth, generated by radioactive decay and the energy of Earth's formation.

GLACIAL   (noun) The cold periods during the Ice Age. (adj.) Having to do with glaciers.

GLACIER   A mass of ice on land, formed from compacted snow, that moves under its own weight.

GLOBAL WARMING   The current warming of the Earth's surface, caused by an increase of greenhouse gases in the atmosphere, especially carbon dioxide.

GRANITE   A type of light-colored, coarse-grained, intrusive igneous rock that is rich in silicon and poor in iron and magnesium. Granite is very common in the continental crust.

GREENHOUSE EFFECT   The absorption and reemission of infrared radiation by greenhouse gases, thereby making the planet warmer than it would otherwise be.

GREENHOUSE GAS   An atmospheric gas that readily absorbs and reemits the infrared radiation given off by the Earth's surface.

GROUNDWATER   Water below the land surface, filling in the open spaces in the soil and rock.

HADLEY CELL   The circulation of air that rises at the equator and descends at 30 degrees latitude.

HALF-LIFE   The time it takes half of the radioactive isotopes to decay. Equivalently, the time in which a single atom has a 50% chance of decaying.

HEADLAND   An extension of land that sticks out into the ocean.

HISTORICAL GEOLOGY   The study of the Earth's history.

HOLOCENE   The epoch that began 10,000 years ago and continues today. Human civilization developed during this time.

HOT SPOT   A fixed plume of hot mantle material that reaches up into the lithosphere.

HYDROLOGIC CYCLE   The movement of water among the reservoirs of the hydrosphere, atmosphere, and biosphere. Also known as the water cycle.

ICE SHEET   A continent-sized glacier.

IGNEOUS ROCK   Rock formed by the solidification, through cooling, of magma.

INFILTRATION   Movement of water downward into soil or porous rock.

INFRARED RADIATION   Light whose wavelength is too long to be seen by the human eye, and which is emitted by all objects with a nonzero absolute temperature.

INTERGLACIAL   The warm periods during an Ice Age.

INTRUSIVE   The term used to describe igneous rock that cooled from magma below Earth's surface.

ISOTOPE   A category of atoms that have the same number of protons and neutrons.

JOINT   A fracture in rock where there has been no movement.

LATITUDE   The distance from the equator, increasing from 0° at the equator to 90° at both the North and South Poles.

LITHIFICATION   The hardening of sediments into rock.

LITHOSPHERE   The hard layer of the Earth, containing the crust, that "floats" on the asthenosphere.

LOAD   The total amount of sediment carried by a stream.

LONGSHORE DRIFT   The zigzag movement of sand up a beach, resulting from waves that strike the shore at an angle.

MAGMA   Hot, molten rock.

MANTLE   The thick, rocky layer of the Earth that sits between the core and the crust.

MASS WASTING   The transfer of rock and soil down a slope under the force of gravity.

MEANDER   A large, loop-like bend in a stream.

METAMORPHIC ROCK   Rock that has been transformed from other rock by heat and/or compression.

METAMORPHISM   A change in the texture and/or chemical composition of rock as a result of high temperatures and/or pressures.

MID-OCEAN RIDGE   A mountainous ridge on the ocean floor that marks the divergent boundary between plates.

MILANKOVITCH THEORY   The proposed explanation for the Ice Age cycles in terms of variations in Earth's orbit caused by the gravitational pull of the other planets.

MINERAL   Any substance that is solid, crystalline, natural, inorganic, and of definite chemical composition.

MORAINE   An accumulation of glacial till either carried within the glacier or deposited in a pile on land.

PHANEROZOIC   The most recent 540 million years of Earth's history, during which life is visible in the fossil record.

PHOTOSYNTHESIS   The process by which plants use sunlight to gather the carbon from carbon dioxide, emitting oxygen in the process.

PHYSICAL GEOLOGY   The study of Earth's physical processes.

PLATE   A continuous piece of lithosphere that moves as a single unit.

PLATE TECTONICS   The theory of plate movement driven by the flow, or convection, of magma in the mantle.

PLEISTOCENE   The epoch that began 1.8 million years ago and ended 10,000 years ago. Humans evolved during this time.

POLAR CELL   The circulation of air that rises at 60 degrees latitude and sinks at 90 degrees latitude.

PRECAMBRIAN   The largest stretch of time in the geologic time scale, from the formation of Earth around 4.6 billion years ago to about 540 million years ago.

PRECIPITATION   Water that falls to the Earth's surface, such as rain or snow.

RADIOACTIVE   A term referring to an atom that has the tendency to spontaneously emit particles from its nucleus.

RADIOCARBON DATING   The method of dating a dead plant or animal by measuring the ratio of ^{14}C to ^{12}C.

ROCK   A natural, solid chunk of minerals, or mineral-like material.

ROCK CYCLE   The cycling of matter among the following five groups: magma, igneous rock, sediment, sedimentary rock, and metamorphic rock.

RUNOFF   Water from precipitation that flows over the surface of the land.

SEA CLIFF   A shoreline cliff formed by wave erosion.

SEAFLOOR SPREADING   New crust formation at the mid-ocean ridges, as explained by Harry Hess.

SEDIMENT   A deposit of fine, loose material.

SEDIMENTARY ROCK   Rock formed from sediments by lithification.

SEISMIC   Having to do with earthquakes.

SHORELINE   The boundary between the land and the sea.

SILICATE   A mineral made out of silicon and oxygen arranged as a pyramid; the silicon atoms sit in the middle of the pyramid and the oxygen atoms lie at the four corners.

SINKHOLE   A depression in the surface caused by the collapse of a cave that was produced by groundwater activity.

SOIL   A mixture of tiny rock particles, weathered minerals, and organic material from dead plants.

STRATOSPHERE   The layer of the atmosphere that ranges from 11 kilometers (6.8 miles) to about 50 kilometers (31 miles).

STRATUM   (plural: strata) A layer of sediments or sedimentary rock.

STREAM   A channeled body of water of any size flowing on the surface.

STRIATION   A groove cut into the bedrock by the scraping action of a moving glacier.

SUBDUCTION ZONE   A convergent margin in which oceanic crust is subducted into the mantle.

SUPERPOSITION   The principle stating that a layer of sedimentary rock is always younger than the layer beneath it.

TEXTURE   The size, shape, and arrangement of the particles that make up a rock.

TILL   The rocks and sediment carried and deposited by a glacier.

TRADE WINDS   The dominant winds near the equator that blow from the east to the west, which result from the Hadley cell circulation and the Coriolis effect.

TRANSFORM FAULT   A margin between two plates that are sliding past each other. No crust is generated or destroyed here.

TROPOSPHERE The layer of the atmosphere from the ground to about 11 kilometers (6.8 miles). This is where all weather takes place.

TSUNAMI An ocean wave produced by an earthquake or some other undersea disturbance, such as a volcanic eruption or landslide.

UNIFORMITARIANISM The theory that Earth's features were formed by the same, slow processes that can be observed at work today.

URBAN SPRAWL The spreading of cities into the surrounding land.

VALLEY GLACIER A glacier that flows down a mountain and through a valley.

VISIBLE SPECTRUM The narrow range of wavelengths at which light is visible by the human eye.

VOLCANIC ARC A string of volcanoes behind a subduction zone that are built from hot material that rises up from the subducting plate.

WATER TABLE The upper surface of the saturated zone.

WAVE HEIGHT The vertical distance between the trough and crest of a wave.

WAVE-CUT PLATFORM A sea-level shelf of rock or debris created by wave erosion on a sea cliff.

WAVELENGTH The horizontal distance between neighboring crests of a wave.

WEATHERING The physical and chemical process by which rocks are broken down into smaller pieces of rock and soil.

BIBLIOGRAPHY

Allègre, C.J., and S.H. Schneider. "The Evolution of the Earth." *Scientific American* (1994): 66–75.

Asner, G.P., A.J. Elmore, L.P. Olander, R.E. Martin, and A.T. Harris. "Grazing Systems, Ecosystem Responses, and Global Change." *Annual Review of Environment and Resources* 29 (2004): 261–299.

Baxter, S. *Revolutions in the Earth: James Hutton and the True Age of the World*. London: Weidenfeld & Nicolson, 2003.

Bridge, G. "Contested Terrain: Mining and the Environment." *Annual Review of Environment and Resources* 29 (2004): 205–259.

Canfield, D. "The Early History of Atmospheric Oxygen: Homage to Robert M. Garrels." *Annual Reviews of Earth and Planetary Science* 33 (2005): 1–36.

Dickey, J., et al. "Lunar Laser Ranging: A Continuing Legacy of the Apollo Program." *Science* 265 (1994): 482–490.

Douglas, I., and N. Lawson. "Material Flows due to Mining and Urbanization." In R.U. Ayres and L.W. Ayres, eds., *A Handbook of Industrial Ecology*, Cheltenham, UK: Edward Elgar, 2000, pp. 351–364.

Engleman, R. *Sustaining Water: Population and the Future of Renewable Water Supplies*. Washington, DC: Population Action International, 1993.

Gleiser, M. "What We Know and What We Don't Know about the Universe." *International Journal of Modern Physics* D13 (2004): 1381–1388.

Goldewijk, K.K. "Estimating Global Land Use Change over the Past 300 Years: The HYDE Database." *Global Biogeochemical Cycles* 15 (2001): 417–433.

Hamblin, W.K., and E.H. Christiansen. *Earth's Dynamic Systems*, 10th ed. Upper Saddle River, NJ: Pearson Education, 2004.

Herring, T.A. "Geodetic Applications of GPS." *Proceedings of the IEEE* 87, no. 1 (1999): 1, 92–110.

Kirshner, R.P. "The Earth's Elements." *Scientific American* (1994): 58–65.

McNeill, J. *Something New Under the Sun: An Environmental History of the Twentieth Century World*. New York: Norton, 2000.

Peebles, J.P., D.N. Schramm, E.L. Turner, and R.G. Kron. "The Evolution of the Universe." *Scientific American* (1994): 52–57.

Press, F., and R. Siever. *Understanding Earth*. New York: W.H. Freeman, 2003.

Repcheck, J. *The Man Who Found Time: James Hutton and the Discovery of the Earth's Antiquity*. New York: Perseus Publishing, 2003.

Skinner, B.J., S.C. Porter, and J. Park, *Dynamic Earth*, 5th ed. New York: John Wiley & Sons, 2004.

Tarbuck, E.J., and F.K. Lutgens. *Earth: An Introduction to Physical Geology*, 6th ed. Upper Saddle River, NJ: Prentice Hall, 1999.

Wetherill, G.W. "Formation of the Earth." *Annual Review of Earth and Planetary Sciences* 18 (1990): 205–256.

Zhang, Y. "The Age and Accretion of the Earth." *Earth-Science Reviews* 59 (2002): 235–263.

FURTHER READING

Allégre, Claude J., and Stephen H. Schneider. "The Evolution of the Earth." *Scientific American* 271 (1994): 66-75.

Bennett, Matthew R., and Neil F. Glasser. *Glacial Geology: Ice Sheets and Landforms.* New York: John Wiley & Sons, 1996.

Bowman, S. *Radiocarbon Dating.* Berkeley: University of California Press, 1990.

Davie, T. *Fundamentals of Hydrology.* New York: Routledge, 2003.

Erickson, Jon. *Glacial Geology: How Ice Shapes the Land.* New York: Facts on File, 1996.

Foley, Jonathan A., et al. "Global Consequences of Land Use." *Science* 309 (2005): 570-574.

Gould, Stephen Jay. *Wonderful Life: The Burgess Shale and Nature of History.* New York: W.W. Norton, 1989.

Gurnis, M. "Sculpting the Earth from Inside Out." *Scientific American* 284 (2001): 40-47.

Hansen, J. "Defusing the Global Warming Time Bomb." *Scientific American* 290 (2004): 68-77.

Herring, T.A. "The Global Positioning System." *Scientific American* 274 (1996): 44-50.

Houghton, John. *Global Warming: The Complete Briefing.* Cambridge: Cambridge University Press, 2004.

Jacob, Daniel. *Introduction to Atmospheric Chemistry.* Princeton, NJ: Princeton University Press, 1999.

Kirshner, Robert P. "The Earth's Elements." *Scientific American* 271 (1994): 58-65.

Lineweaver, C.H., and T.M. Davis. "Misconceptions about the Big Bang." *Scientific American* 292 (2005): 36-45.

MacDougall, J.D. *A Short History of Planet Earth: Mountains, Mammals, Fire and Ice.* John Wiley & Sons, 1996.

MacDougall, J.D., *Frozen Earth: The Once and Future Story of Ice Ages.* Berkeley: University of California Press, 2004.

Pinter, N., and M.T. Brandon. "How Erosion Builds Mountains." *Scientific American* 276 (1997): 74-79.

Taylor, S. Ross, and Scott M. McClennan. "The Evolution of Continental Crust." *Scientific American* 274 (1996): 76-81.

Vitousek, Peter M., et al. "Human Domination of Earth's Ecosystems." *Science* 277 (1997): 494-499.

York, Derek. "The Earliest History of the Earth." *Scientific American* 268 (1993): 90-96.

Web Sites

Global River Discharge Database
http://www.sage.wisc.edu/riverdata/

GPS Time Series
http://sideshow.jpl.nasa.gov/mbh/series.html

National Hurricane Center
http://www.nhc.noaa.gov

Nova and Frontline Examine the Truth about Global Warming
http://www.pbs.org/wgbh/warming/

Real-time Earthquake Maps
http://quake.wr.usgs.gov/recent/index.html

Real-time Groundwater Levels in the U.S.
http://waterdata.usgs.gov/nwis/gw

Swiss Glacier Monitoring Network
http://glaciology.ethz.ch/swiss-glaciers/

This Dynamic Earth
http://pubs.usgs.gov/publications/text/dynamic.html

PICTURE CREDITS

INDEX

ABOUT THE AUTHOR

DAVID M. THOMPSON is an Environmental Fellow at the Center for the Environment at Harvard University. He was previously a postdoctoral fellow at Harvard University's Department of Earth and Planetary Sciences and the Woods Hole Research Center. Dr. Thompson holds bachelor's and master's degrees in physics from Yale University and a Ph.D. in theoretical particle physics from Harvard University. His postdoctoral research includes work on atmospheric physics as well as energy technology and climate change policy. Dr. Thompson has taught as an adjunct professor of physics at Suffolk University.

ABOUT THE EDITOR

DAVID G. HAASE is Professor of Physics and Director of The Science House at North Carolina State University. He earned a B.A. in physics and mathematics at Rice University and an M.A. and Ph.D. in physics at Duke University, where he was a J.B. Duke Fellow, and has been an active researcher in experimental low temperature and nuclear physics. Dr. Haase is the founding Director of The Science House (www.science-house.org), which annually serves over 3,000 teachers and 20,000 students across North Carolina. He has co-authored over 120 papers in experimental physics and in science education, and has co-edited one book of student learning activities and five volumes of Conference Proceedings on K-12 Outreach from University Science Departments. Dr. Haase has received the Distinguished Service Award of the North Carolina Science Teachers Association and was chosen 1990 Professor of the Year in the State of North Carolina by the Council for the Advancement and Support of Education (CASE).